MW01205952

Eye on the Caribou

**Also by Chris Carlson**


*Cecil Andrus: Idaho's Greatest Governor* (Caxton)

*Medimont Reflections* (Ridenbaugh)


Unpublished:

*The Intercession of St. Dismas:*
    *A Personal History*

*A Short History of the Gallatin Group*

# Eye on the Caribou

## Inside the Alaska Lands Bill

Chris Carlson

Foreword by Governor Cecil D. Andrus

**Ridenbaugh Press**
**Carlton, Oregon**

Copyright © 2015 Chris Carlson
All Rights Reserved.
No part of this book may be reproduced, stored in a retrieval system, or transmitted in any form by any means, without prior permission of the publisher.

Composition and editing by Ridenbaugh Press, Carlton, Oregon.
Cover design by Randy Stapilus.

Library of Congress Cataloging-in-Publication Data:

Carlson, Chris
    Eye of the Caribou: Inside the Alaska Lands Bill
    ISBN 978-0-945648-28-4 (softbound)
    1. Alaska. 2. Politics 3. Environment 4. Business. I. Title.


Printed in the United States of America.
August 2015
10 9 8 7 6 5 4 3 2 1


Photo of Wallace MacGregor by Serena Carlson
Photo of Chuck Gilbert by National Park Service

# CONTENTS

Timeline

Author's note                                                    1

Foreword *by Cecil D. Andrus*                                    4


Part One:  Legislation


1  Flying In                                                    25

2  In the Country                                               34

3  Oil Politics                                                 49

4  People, Debate, Passage                                      72


Part Two:  Consequences


5  Early Diggings                                              120

6  Orange Hill                                                 129

7  Lawyers and Lobbyists                                       157

8  To the Rescue?                                              168

9  The Four Horsemen


Acknowledgments                                                196

Correspondence                                                 199

Appendices                                                     204

Appendix A:  The Alaskan Lands Hall of Heroes

Appendix B:  Bibliography

Appendix C:  About the author

*Dedication*

To the Four Horsemen of the Alaska Lands Legislation.

The quarterback, Cecil D. Andrus, who drove the team the last 20 yards through the Red Zone to the winning touchdown;

The slot back, Chuck Clusen, head of the Alaska Coalition, who kept the team together and focused;

The halfback, Brock Evans, from the Sierra Club, who could block or run with anyone; and,

The fullback, Doug Scott, from the Wilderness Society, the lead lobbyist every day, the three yards and a cloud of dust, nitty gritty tough one.

All four made up the *sine qua non*. May a grateful nation never forget.

# Author's note

A brief note on the origins of this book.

My first goal in writing this book was to make sure a critical element in the sterling legacy of former four-term Idaho governor and U.S. Secretary of the Interior Cecil D. Andrus – his key role in one of the greatest accomplishments legislatively for any presidential administration in history – was duly noted and properly recorded. Andrus deserves the credit for the indispensable role he played, and I felt the story of that role should be easily found in book form for researchers and future historians.

I also view this book as the completion of a trilogy of sorts. My first book was a biography of Governor Andrus (*Cecil Andrus: Idaho's Greatest Governor*) and my second (*Medimont Reflections*) included several essays specifically dealing with other Andrus accomplishments that had not received their due in the previous book, such as his work on the Hells Canyon and Sawtooth National Recreation areas.

Together these books are intended to give a future reader or researcher or historian a sense of the considerable accomplishments of one of this nation's truly most gifted and remarkable politicians.

I'd also felt that the Alaska Coalition, led by three remarkable individuals, all of whom had worked for the Sierra Club at one time or another, had, like Andrus, never received their proper attention. These three – Chuck Clusen, Brock Evans, and Doug Scott – formed an unusually good partnership with Andrus, worked well together and succeeded because they wanted the goal and cared little about who got the credit.

There's a secondary story here as well, one that details the efforts of one individual and his relationship with the newly created Wrangell-St. Elias National Park and Preserve which surrounded his property. The property owner, Wallace McGregor, framed his demands as a case reflecting whether private property rights were still observed in this country. This second story also demonstrates that something viewed almost universally as a good and great accomplishment can be something quite different for others.

The stories demonstrate a symbiotic relationship. In describing one's adverse impact from the legislation, I hope the reader comes to a better understanding that what happens in D.C. really does matter and does have real life impacts.

*Chris Carlson*
*Medimont, Idaho*
*May 30, 2015*

P.S. Some readers may wonder about the book's title.

One of Governor Andrus' frequently heard exhortations to his staff was: Keep your eye on the rabbit. By that he meant it was important to stay focused on the goal.

I decided to amend the statement by inserting the word "caribou" because in many respects the Porcupine caribou herd and its unimpeded migration route have become symbolic of what the Alaskan lands legislation was all about: Preserving entire eco-systems in their virginal state unmarked by man. This is especially true with regard to the on-going debate over how much of the huge Arctic National Refuge should be classified as wilderness in part to ensure there is never any drilling for oil and gas. Caribou is a word that connotes Alaska. Thus, the title.

Others may also question the inclusion of McGregor's 1953 float trip on the Coleen River with Ed Owens. It is included because it demonstrates the Alaskan spirit as personified by both McGregor and Owens. Their sense of adventure, their fearlessness, their fortitude in the face of the challenge the Alaskan landscape can confront one with is inspiring. It's a reminder of the pioneer movement which brought so many West in the 19th century.

The human side of the Alaska lands story is important. A piece of legislation that looks great when viewed in the abstract nonetheless has real life impacts when implemented on the ground and in the field.

*Cecil D. Andrus, 44th Secretary of the Interior, 26th and 28th governor of Idaho*

# Foreword

*by Cecil D. Andrus*

Some will recall that I had the privilege and honor to serve our nation not just in the United States Navy (from 1951 to 1955), during the Korean War, but also as President Jimmy Carter's Secretary of the Interior (from 1977 to 1981).

The number one item on President Carter's legislative agenda for the Interior department was to pass successfully into law the long promised set aside of over 100 million acres of pristine land to be protected in perpetuity by designation as wilderness areas, national parks, national wildlife refuges, national monuments and as wild and scenic rivers.

The requirement for Congress to enact this unprecedented set aside in Alaska was contained in Sections 17-d-1 and 17-d-2 of the Alaska Native Claims Settlement Act (ANCSA). This legislation had been passed to resolve the legitimate land claims of Alaska's Natives and Eskimos. These native claims had to be resolved before construction could start on the trans-Alaska pipeline designed to carry crude oil and gas from Alaska's North Slope to the ice free port of Valdez on the southern coast of Alaska. It was a promise to Alaska's Natives as well as the nation's environmental community and indeed all Alaskans that there would be a remunerative quid pro quo for allowing the pipeline construction to proceed. For the State of Alaska it would lead to the unfreezing of federal lands and would allow state land selections promised in the 1958 Statehood Act.

For all the interested parties it was a classic "bet on the come."

The Act gave Congress approximately seven years in which to comply with the d-2 language.

Some credit me with master-minding the strategy that ultimately brought about the successful passage of the legislation.

I don't deny that I played a critical role, but I also recognize there are hundreds, if not thousands, whose work we built upon, going back to John Muir, President Theodore Roosevelt, and the first U.S. Forest Service chief, Gifford Pinchot.

They recognized that Alaska contained vast ecosystems essentially unmarked and untrammeled by man; that true wilderness was rapidly shrinking; and, that Alaska represented America's last, best chance to preserve this unique legacy. Each in his way worked for the goal of protecting this incredible American asset. We were given the chance to do it right the first time.

Progress was incremental and slow at times. Ultimately, though, there was a critical mass of proponents across the nation who, with the guidance of key folks within Interior, helped to achieve passage of the Alaska lands legislation.

I've often used the football analogy to describe my role and President Carter's. He was the head coach. I was the quarterback who could change the play without checking with the coach. My "quarterback coach" was Cynthia Wilson, who headed up the small but powerful internal Alaskan Task Force I put together to oversee the Interior Department's handling of this critical issue.

The result was we were able to carry the ball through the red zone to score the winning touchdown.

Success has a thousand fathers; failure is a bastard.

This book is about the history and process leading to passage of the Alaska lands legislation. It is also about the Law of Unintended Consequences: How a law, good for the many, turned out to be a life-altering event for one of several individuals. As co-owners of a patented, fully proved up private property, Wallace McGregor and his partners' constitutional right to be compensated for a taking has never been accomplished despite their property becoming surrounded by the creation of the Wrangell-St. Elias National Park. Whose fault this is I'll leave the reader to decide, but at times it appeared to me both parties talked past each other and began to question each other's motives. That is not a good formula for successful resolution.

The issue remains unresolved, however, and for it to fester for 35 years just does not seem right. The lead individual, Wallace McGregor, has every right to receive fair compensation, as do his partners. Trying to define "fair compensation" lies at the heart of their differences. Incontestably, it has been 35 years, however, since they lost beneficial use of their property. Expectations of justice and equity ebb with each day as McGregor approaches his 90th birthday.

Readers of both these stories will see no simple case of right or wrong, black or white. Like all tough conflicts, especially those between conflicting rights, there are layers of complexities and ambiguities. Neither party will have a monopoly on the truth and the right.

The bottom line for me, though, is I also believe ANILCA's passage reflects the greatest good for the greatest number. It will stand the test of time and at the end of the day I think most will see that the National Park Service understands the Constitution as well as McGregor or anyone else and does its best to fulfill its mission within the boundaries of that great document.

Finally, I want to add my own words of praise and thanks for the three key leaders of the Alaska Coalition – Chuck Clusen, Brock Evans and Doug Scott. Their roles were critical, some would argue even more critical than mine. Together we succeeded and we all relish and will forever cherish our opportunity to be one of the many fathers and mothers of the Alaskan lands legislation.

*Cecil D. Andrus*
*Boise, Idaho*
*May 15, 2015*

# Timeline

*By Cynthia Wilson*
*Executive Director, Secretary Andrus' Alaskan Lands*
*Departmental Task Force*

**1968** Oil struck at Prudhoe Bay.

**1971** Passage of the Alaska Native Claims Settlement Act laid the groundwork for this legislation. It set a deadline of December 1978 when protection of the d-2 lands would end.

**1976** Congress passes the Federal Land Policy and Management Act (FLPMA) which would play an important part in protecting the land after Congress failed to pass legislation.

**1976** The Alaska Coalition, comprised of all the environmental groups and other nonprofits, was formed. Key organizations: National Audubon Society, Wilderness Society, Sierra Club, NRDC, National Parks & Conservation Association Friends of the Earth.

Coalition drafted what became the original H.R. 39 protecting more than 100 million acres.

**January 1977** Introduction of H.R. 39 by Congressman Morris Udall and numerous co-sponsors. Field hearings by new Alaska subcommittee, chaired by Rep. John Seiberling, launched.

Secretary Andrus pledges to review the recommendations developed by Secretary Morton and report to Congress with recommendations by September.

**Early summer 1977** Secretary Andrus chairs a decision meeting. This brought objections from Energy and Commerce Departments during OMB review. President Carter backed Interior on this issue. The Alaska lands legislation became the Administration's top environmental priority.

Secretary Andrus presented the recommendations to House Interior Committee in September with strong support from the Alaska Coalition. The State espoused legislation with small park and refuge areas surrounded by lands which would be "cooperatively managed by state and federal government."

**1978** During House Committee markup, Rep. Don Young offers numerous amendments delaying the bill.

**May 19, 1978** The measure passes the House by 277-31 votes.

**June 1978** Concerned about the lack of Senate action, the Department begins preparing a Supplemental Environmental Impact Statement. The Secretary warned Congress and the State that administrative action was possible if the legislation did not pass.

**Summer 1978** The Secretary and press visit the proposed parks and refuges hoping to increase pressure on the Senate committee.

**October 4** The Senate Energy committee reports out the bill but it was not acceptable to the Administration, House leaders and the Coalition.

**October 12** Senator Gravel announces he would not stand in the way if agreement could be reached.

**October 13** An "ad hoc" conference is held.

**October 15** The principals agree to a one year extension, but on the Senate floor Gravel shoots it down by announcing a filibuster. Later that day, Congress adjourned.

**October 17** The Draft Supplemental EIS was sent to the printers, then released for a 30 day comment period.

**October 30** State filed suit to block administrative actions.

**November 7** Congressional elections.

**November 14** Despite assurances from Governor Jay Hammond, the state files selections within the boundaries of the proposed parks and refuges.

**November 16** Secretary uses Sec. 204 of FLPMA to withdraw 110 million acres – all the land Congress had been considering -- for 3 years.

**November 23** Over Thanksgiving weekend, Interior staff finalized Supplemental EIS.

**November 24** U.S. District Court in Alaska denied the state's request for a TRO, saying that Andrus had acted legally and freeing him to make a recommendation to the President about using the Antiquities Act. This had some risk that Congress might repeal the Act, but Andrus believed the risk was worth taking.

**December 1, 1978** President designates 56 million acres as national monuments. He also directs the Secretary to take the legal steps necessary to designate the balance as national wildlife refuges should the new Congress fail to act of the d-2 legislation.

**May 1979** The full House passes a strong bill by 360-65, but once again the bill bogged down in the Senate. Senator Paul Tsongas (D-MA) joined the Energy Committee and became the advocate for the administration and coalition.

**November 1, 1979** Committee reports a bill that was still unacceptable to Admin and coalition, and Tsongas introduces a substitute bill.

At the President's direction, Interior prepares necessary legal documentation to put remainder of proposed lands in permanent refuge status should the bill again bog down, so all work is completed in fiscal year and locked in a safe.

**February 1980** Senator Gravel (up for re-election) persuades Majority Leader Senator Robert Byrd (D-W.Va) to delay floor action until after 4th of July.

**February 11** As threatened, Secretary by executive order establishes some 40 million acres as national wildlife refuges.

**June 26** Judge rules from the bench in favor of the Administration, blowing Gravel's argument that the lawsuit will get rid of the national monuments. Bill comes up after fourth of July recess, Gravel filibusters, cloture is invoked. Debate over Tsongas amendments becomes so bitter that Byrd pulls the bill from the floor and tells both sides to work something out.

**August 19** Negotiations produce a new compromise which Jackson and Tsongas offer, with silent acquiescence of Stevens. Compromise passes easily, and Gravel loses his primary.

The Coalition and Udall continue to push for additional concessions from the Senate. Senate concessions are rejected by House; Stevens walks out. Relations between Coalition and the Administration are at the breaking point; the Coalition is splintering.

**November** Under pressure from Secretary Andrus, Coalition concedes. Technical amendments delay the bill.

**December 1** The bill reaches the White House.

**December 2** President Carter signs the bill.

*Various shades of grays, greens and browns delineate the over 100 million acres of Alaskan lands added to America's great system of National Parks, National Wildlife Refuges, National Monuments and Wilderness Areas, as well as Wild and Scenic rivers added on December 2, 1980. Map by National Park Service.*

# Part One

# Legislation

# Introduction

*President Jimmy Carter (left, facing front) fishing on the Middle Fork of the Salmon River with Interior Secretary Andrus and their wives in August of 1978. Photo courtesy of the Carter Library.*

How did Wallace McGregor, a New Jersey-born kid, become an exploration geologist roaming the great Alaska frontier with his wife, Darlene Dorwert, a Colorado native, beside him?

It was a straight forward question that might have darted around a late August campfire beside Idaho's Middle Fork of the Salmon River in the summer of 2012, as McGregor and his family visited the great Idaho wilderness.

Rafting the Middle Fork is a true wilderness experience. There are no roads running along side of the river. The only noise of any machine one may hear is that of a jet high overhead flying between Spokane and Boise or Spokane and Salt Lake. If one of the overnight camping spots is near the Flying B Ranch, one may hear an occasional Cessna 182 or Cessna 206 flying up or down the river, depending on wind direction, before landing at the "B" to unload fly fishermen or hunters.

All professional wilderness guide services, like the service guiding the McGregors, practice "no-trace camping." This means they carry large fire pans for the evening campfire so critical to the ambiance of a wilderness float trip. After the morning breakfast is done, the guides remove the fire pan along with any remaining coals. In a like manner guides set up a short distance from camp a "wilderness WC," and remove all human waste that may have been deposited while at the camp site.

Before leaving, guides and guests comb the camp site and remove any sign of their presence. They make sure no gum wrappers or bottle caps mar the camp site. More than 10,000 people a year pay over a thousand dollars a head to take the trip. Because of the care displayed by guides, it seems like a virginal trip to everyone who travels the river.

The joy of being in the wilderness, far from madding crowds, a place where cell phones are out of range and blackberries are for eating, not sending e-mail, creates a sense of a shared experience that is the perfect antidote for many to the frenetic pace of their normal lives. The setting, the fire, the peacefulness that creeps into one's soul reinforces for most the need to protect and preserve these places for future generations to enjoy.

Rafting and floating these great rivers is not only exhilarating when shooting rapids, they also provide tranquil moments when one relaxes so quickly and so easily they can all too easily fall into a deep slumber.

For some, the key element for enjoying a backcountry, wilderness experience is sitting around a camp fire after dinner is done and the clean-up is over with. Guides and guests usually have a wee bit of some libation, and folks often have donned a light jacket or a polar-tec to blunt the edge of a cool wind gently blowing downstream. Staring into the flames puts folks in both a pensive and expansive mode as the conversation leaps from topic to topic.

It was a once-in-a-lifetime experience for the McGregor family, but for all the appreciation of the wilderness country, the occasion was bittersweet. McGregor was still mourning the January 2011 loss of his beloved wife of 55 years. He saw the trip as a continuation of the healing process, though he knew the hole in his heart would never close.

McGregor may have pondered too other questions, about a property called Orange Hill he had bought in another wild country far to the north in Alaska, only to see his beneficial use of it – for mining – closed off by the federal government.

That loss might be considered an "unintended consequence" of the passage of something called the "d-2 Alaska lands legislation," which, overnight, surrounded his property with a new national park and a park preserve called the Wrangell-St. Elias. This new park became the single largest national park in the nation, comprising a land area the size of Switzerland – in excess of 13.2 million acres.

But how did it happen? Did it have to happen?

McGregor could have had no way of knowing that the fate of his Orange Hill mining property and the resolution of other Alaska lands issues was, in one of those ironic coincidences that history sometimes provides, in large part decided thirty-four years earlier on another Middle Fork raft trip, along this same river.


The participants in that other Middle Fork trip, more than three decades earlier in August 1978 included the 39th president of the

United States, Jimmy Carter, and his wife, Rosalynn, and their hosts, Secretary of the Interior Cecil D. Andrus, and his wife, Carol.

Andrus, while still serving as Idaho's governor in November of 1976, had extended an invitation to the then president-elect to take a fly fishing float trip on Idaho's Middle Fork of the Salmon. Andrus issued the invitation while standing in the Carters' kitchen at their home in Plains, following his interview to be the next Secretary of the Interior. Carter accepted the invitation from the incoming 44th Interior secretary, and he kept his word.

The float trip turned out to be both serendipitous and fortuitous. As the two couples sat around the evening fire, the men would first settle up on the day's bet regarding who caught and released the most cutthroat, the largest and the first. They usually bet $1 on each. And then the conversation would turn to larger matters.

The timing could not have been better. Just a month earlier Andrus had taken 15 of the nation's premier journalists on a week-long tour of Alaska covering many of the sites being contemplated as additions to the nation's great systems of protection and conservation: wilderness, national parks, national wildlife refuges, national monuments and the wild and scenic rivers system. The trip garnered extensive publicity for setting aside and protecting anywhere from 80 million to 103 million acres of federal lands. This would satisfy the commitment to the environmental community to accept the settlement of the long unresolved land claims of Alaska's natives. It also allowed the trans-Alaska pipeline to proceed in exchange for a promised significant increase in the great preservation and conservation programs that over the years the United States, more by luck than coordinated planning, has been able to achieve.

With his Alaska trip fresh in his mind, and knowing that the president's number one goal for the nation's major environmental organizations was passage of the Alaska lands legislation, Andrus took full advantage of time spent by the evening camp fire to discuss his media tour of Alaska, the status of the then negotiations, the likelihood that Alaska's Democratic Senator,

Mike Gravel, would prove to be the dog in the manger and do everything he could to stall and delay any legislation.

Always able to look down the road and over the horizon to anticipate what would be coming, Andrus began to lay out his fall-back strategy to the president should Gravel not only succeed in torpedoing the current legislation being proposed but also block an extension of the deadline for resolution of the lands issue contained in the 1971 Land Claims Act.

The idea involved achieving the goal by using the presidential land withdrawal power under the Antiquities Act to create national monuments by the stroke of a pen. Andrus thought President Carter might have to designate as many as 17 new or expanded national monuments to protect both the lands and congress' option to act in compliance with the previous Alaska Native Claims Settlement Act requirement.

Andrus had the complete trust of the president. The two had worked closely together when both were serving as governor of their respective states and became acquainted at National Governor Association meetings. In later years Carter would say Andrus was the only person he considered for the Interior post. He relied heavily on Andrus' views with regards to most western issues and backed up every decision Andrus later made on Alaska.

Andrus had been reading about Alaska since childhood, in particular Jack London's stories about Alaska and the Yukon. He also fondly recalled that the barbershop in the nearest town to their little farm used to save the old *Outdoor Life* magazines, and he and his brother, Steve, would read every issue from cover to cover, and dream about some day visiting there.

Andrus said that what initially intrigued him about Alaska was the huge bears on Kodiak Island. He was fascinated by the stories of moose hunting, of migrating caribou, of the great glaciers.

Keep in mind, he told the president, that here was a 10-year-old boy, looking at the pictures of big moose, big bears, hunters, wide open spaces and mighty glaciers. Looming over it all was the massive Mt. McKinley, the highest mountain in North America.

Andrus told the president that he had just never seen anything like it. It represented the wild because it was unsettled and impressive beyond belief.

# 1

# Flying in

*Flying into the Walker Lake area. Photo by National Park Service.*

In the late fall of 1953 the owners of Kennecott, the giant copper producing company, received at their offices an unsolicited letter from a man named Ed Owens.

Owens was a loner, a man usually unlikely to be anywhere near the radar screen of a corporate giant. He was trapper, gold prospector and miner, living not just in Alaska but in an extremely remote part of what still was a territory, not even a state: on the Coleen River well above the Arctic Circle, over 100 miles northeasterly from Fort Yukon. His type—independent, opinionated, loud, proud, and hard-working—was well described by John McPhee in his classic book on Alaska, *Coming Into the Country*.

Owens could have easily been the gyppo miner living alone deep in the wilderness instead of Richard Okeh "Dick" Cook, the classic wilderness dweller interviewed instead by McPhee. There are several hundred individuals throughout Alaska like them, unique characters who share similar characteristics.

In his letter to Kennecott, Owen explained that during the course of several decades prospecting the area, he had seen areas of mineralization and offered to show the prospects to the company. The offer drew interest at the company. A newly hired employee and recent graduate of the Colorado School of Mines, Wallace McGregor, was assigned to evaluate the finds.

In the early 1950s there was no geologic reconnaissance by helicopter. This had some benefit to McGregor, because the experience Owens had to offer went well beyond a strictly geologic investigation. With the exception of relying on a bush plane to reach the area to be explored, their means of transportation were as basic as traversing the tundra with pack-dogs and floating the Coleen River on log rafts. It was a unique opportunity to trek the Arctic with a true prospector of a bygone era. McGregor jumped at the opportunity.

Kennecott management decided to send an additional geologist as well. He was Jim Bright, a Colorado School of Mines classmate of McGregor's, who had hired on as a summer employee.

Their plan was to fly by bush plane from Fort Yukon to Owens' cabin, pick up Owens, and from there fly to the northernmost reach of the Coleen River, landing on a river gravel bar from which they would trek to the prospect sites and return to the river to be picked up on an appointed day.

Arriving at Fort Yukon, McGregor and Bright were surprised to be met by Owens, who explained that he had become concerned about communications because his only means was by letter delivered by plane every two weeks. As a consequence, he decided to float the Coleen to the Porcupine River and on to Fort Yukon. The boat was homemade. Owens had brought his two huskies with him for packing their food and cooking gear.

The resourcefulness of this Alaskan original was immediately apparent as Owens explained how he had managed to survive in isolation in an unforgiving environment for so many years. At the time of their meeting, Owens was 72 years old, placing him at the age of a young man in the first decade of the '98 gold rush. How and when Owens "came into the country," and then wound up on the Coleen River, McGregor never found out. Many come to Alaska because they believe they can start over and leave their past behind, and see little point to talking about how and when. One is to accept them as they are.

He did, though, show McGregor and Bright a 4th of July picture taken in the gold rush town of Nome. He guessed that was sometime around the turn of the century and validated that the old boy really was in his 70s.

Owens told them he had married a native woman, as some of the gyppo miners and fur trappers do to have a cook and companionship during the long winters. Their relationship ended when his wife left him, taking off in his boat and floating down to Fort Yukon in the same manner that Owens had for their meeting. He also mentioned having raised a daughter, who was living elsewhere in Alaska at the time of their meeting, but with whom he remained in contact.

Owens' decision to meet in Fort Yukon proved wise in that it provided the opportunity to better plan and coordinate with the bush pilot who was to fly them to their destination, returning later to pick them up.

The initial decision on where to begin exploration was made, and it was for McGregor and Bright to start the prospecting with Owens' guidance on the upper Coleen, more than 100 river miles from the confluence with the Porcupine River as their first step. This was close to 200 miles northeast of Fort Yukon. Then they would work their way southerly down the river.

Three men, two pack dogs, food, related supplies and camping gear is quite a bit of material and "animals" (human as well as canine) to pack into a bush plane, but they managed by using a back country workhorse, the vaunted Norseman. It only took one trip, but as it lumbered down the runway and slowly lifted into the air all three had to wonder if the plane was really going to fly.

Owens claimed he had prospected all the way north to the Romanov Mountains of the Brooks Range. So, they flew as far north up the Coleen River as the availability of gravel bars made landing possible. This was of course a matter of judgment by the bush pilot, but they were confident of his capability. Prominently posted inside the plane was a little plaque with the saying in Alaska, "There are old pilots, and there are bold pilots. There are no old, bold pilots!"

They landed on a gravel bar on the opposite side of the river from their destination, which was not a problem because of the river's low level at the time. That would not be the case 10 days later when they returned to the river for pick up. Several days of rain had put the gravel landing bar under water. This dictated they try to find some sort of landing strip further downstream and surely compounded a sense of frustration given the challenges encountered as they tried to follow the prospecting route taken earlier by Owens.

They were north of the tree line, and the mosquito infestation was heavy. For anyone who has fished, hiked or hunted in Alaska, it is easy to imagine what they encountered and the need to constantly wear the mosquito net headgear to keep from feeling they were about to be eaten alive.

Getting to the first mineralization site required crossing miles of tundra, which was not an easy task because they were walking in mud between intermittent islands of grass. Onward they plodded though, the two young bucks marveling at the ease with which Ed Owens handled all the challenges they faced.

When the party reached the first mineralization, the two geology majors found it to be disseminated sphalerite and not of particular interest, especially given the remoteness.

Inasmuch as their first objective had been obtained with plenty of time to spare, they decided to climb a nearby mountain. It was not a difficult climb. When they reached the summit they were surprised to find that the top was flat, strewn with angular rocks of varied size. This raised the question of cause, which, in short order, was answered.

As they looked to the west down range, they saw a thunderstorm heading their way with lightning striking on one of the nearest peaks. As McGregor raised his geology pick to point, it began to buzz. At the same time the wind came up and it began to rain. They wisely decided to take cover behind some rocks off the top of the mountain on its leeward side opposite their access route off the peak.

After a while, with the rain showing no signs of letting up, they decided to head down off the mountain by taking the route back over the top. As they did, everything started buzzing, including McGregor's geology pick which he had pocketed on his side, and the mosquito netting on his head. The mountain top was charged with electricity.

Anyone who has hiked mountain ridges during the hot month of August, whether in Alaska or Idaho or Washington, can easily imagine the feeling of vulnerability to an imminent lightning strike. In particular, when one feels the static electricity causing the hair on their arms to stand up, and can also smell the ozone in the air, they know they are truly at the mercy of the elements.

McGregor began to understand, however, the explanation for the flat mountain top: The peak was so prone to lightning strikes that over the centuries it had blasted the top into flatness since it usually struck whatever happened to be the highest point at the time.

They managed to get off the mountain safely, but the rains proved to be the beginning of a long storm. The result was the Coleen River rose, flooding their landing strip.

They quickly set out to find a higher elevation gravel bar, but all were strewn with debris which necessitated clearing, often by hand, in order to create a landing strip. When the bush plane returned, they had cleared a minimal length strip for a landing. The pilot managed to land but with a smaller plane than the one he used to fly them in; it took three trips to haul the men, dogs and gear back downstream for their first visit to Owens' cabin.

McGregor and Bright were surprised and much impressed by Owens' cabin, which he had single-handedly created for himself. McGregor's recollection is that the cabin was approximately twenty feet wide by thirty feet long. McGregor was especially impressed at how Owens managed to get the roof beams in place. Even though he carefully explained the process, McGregor would tell those listening to his story how difficult it was to visualize one man doing it all by himself.

One of McGregor's most vivid memories was the huge bear rug that covered the center of the floor. When asked if there was a story behind the rug, the old trapper instead told a story about having fallen through the ice on the river during a return from a trapping run. Luckily, Owens managed to get out of the water and back to his cabin. He quickly shed his frozen clothes, in the course of which he walked around bare footed on the bear rug while getting the fire started. What he didn't take into consideration was that the bear skin was as freezing cold as the floor: he wound up with frost-bitten feet.

The three prospectors' plan was to continue by raft down the Coleen River from Owens' cabin, examining shows of mineralization along the way, hiking from the river. They planned to wind up at the confluence of the Coleen and Porcupine rivers, where their bush pilot would again pick them up.

To make the river trip Owens said, they would need to build two rafts from scratch. When pressed to say why they needed two, the old curmudgeon said he didn't want to be on the same

raft with two guys who didn't know how to raft. McGregor and
Bright could see his reasoning.

His point was well-taken; "sweepers" or "widow-makers," trees
that had tipped out into the water from cut banks could be deadly. If
a raft were to get carried under the sweepers, not only could
everything on the raft (including the oarsman) be swept off, but the
raft could flip, trapping the passengers beneath it where their
chances of rescue are minimal.

To make his point about the need to stay clear of sweepers,
Owens told McGregor and Bright a story about two kayakers who
wound up at his cabin one autumn evening. They were kayaking the
Coleen and had been swept under some sweepers  losing
everything, kayak included. They had no means of communication,
but did know the whereabouts of Owens' cabin. All they could hope
to do to survive was to hike down the river to his cabin, which
fortunately was within a couple of days' hike.

After the discussion about rafting safety, it was time to start the
raft-building. The materials were close at hand – some pine trees
near Owens' cabin that he had planned to use as a source of dry
firewood. They were ideal for raft building and Owens was well
versed in the craft. Two rafts were built with adequate heft and
soundness to support the weight of Owens, the huskies and a share
of the supplies on one, and Bright and McGregor and the remaining
supplies on the other.

Before launching, Owens instructed the two men on the
technique necessary to navigate the flow of the river to avoid the
sweepers – the key principle being to keep on the inside of the curve
of the river flow. McGregor and Bright took the instructions
seriously and spent time practicing how to guide the raft using long
poles. As a result, they kept out of harm's way for the entire rafting
trip.

Once underway, at Owens' instruction, they would pull in to
beach the rafts, pack up the dogs and head out for as much as
several days of hiking through the bush to a mineral show. They
visited prospective placer gold deposits that Owens had worked,
sinking shafts during the winter in order to avoid the permafrost
thawing while he dug the test shafts. He then prevented the shafts

from thawing during the summer by covering them well with brush.

One afternoon as they came around a bend in the Coleen a pack of wolves faced them on a gravel bar. In the summer of 1954 there was a bounty on wolves. Owens quickly grabbed his rifle and shot one. The rest of the pack ran into the bush. For proof of a kill, in order to satisfy Alaska Fish and Game, it was necessary to remove a shin bone from the wolf carcass. While Owens was performing the bone removal, the wolf pack started howling in the distance, clearly saying good-bye to their companion.

McGregor said, years later, he would never forget the haunting sound. He would tell others that it made it difficult for him to sit through the movie, *Never Cry Wolf*, based on the book by Farley Mowat, because the movie put great emphasis on the family orientation of the wolf pack.

Rather than sit all day on the raft, Bright and McGregor would take turns navigating while the other hiked along the river. On one occasion, Bright was ashore at the time that they decided to beach and set up camp for the night. They gave Bright a call and shortly thereafter he came out of the brush on the opposite shore. As Bright was wading across the stream out of the brush behind him came a bear.

Whether the bear was stalking Bright, or just appeared, Owens took no chances, grabbed his rifle quickly and with one shot killed the bear. McGregor and Bright, still feeling the adrenaline rush, nonetheless thought the huskies, whose diet was dried fish, would like some fresh meat. So, they cut out some meat from the bear and placed it in front of the dogs. Their reaction was to pull as far away from the bear meat as their leashes would allow. They wanted no part of it.

Within a few days of their planned pick-up rendezvous with the bush plane near the confluence of the Coleen and the Porcupine rivers, Owens showed them an interesting copper mineralization prospect right on the river. McGregor quickly set about mapping the geology, but when it became clear there wasn't the time to complete the mapping, they decided to send Owens ahead to meet the plane while McGregor finished the geologic mapping. When the plane arrived, Owens would direct the pilot to their location.

That plan worked as intended. They completed the mapping and sampling, and had enough time to do something extra. In this case, it was climbing up to a peregrine falcon nest on a cliff overlooking the river. The nest had two chicks. During the couple of extra days they were there, McGregor visited the nest on several occasions to take pictures. The falcon parents were not very happy with his presence and bombarded him with dead mice.

On the appointed day for the pickup flight, Bright and McGregor were packed and ready to go when the sound of the approaching Norseman was heard flying at low level up the river. When the plane came into view they waved and with that, the pilot did a wing dip in recognition, made a turn around and landed to pick them up. They loaded their back packs and samples on board and left the rafts to be washed down the river in the due course of the next high water.

When McGregor and Bright parted company with Owens in Fort Yukon two days later, they knew they would in all probability never see him again. The parting thus contained a note of regret and sadness. While McGregor and Bright had not observed any mineralization worthy of follow up, both knew they owed Owens "a big one." He had introduced them to an experience that served to heighten McGregor's intrigue with the concept of "Land of Tomorrow" and his desire to be a part of the future it represented.

# 2

# In the country

*An Alaskan sunset (photo courtesy the National Oceanic and Atmospheric Administration)*

Alaska is vast:

568,422 square miles.

Almost 375 million acres.

Four time zones.

With a population of 730,000 people spread over an area whose vastness is unimaginable, what is surprising is the urban/rural split: It is 64% urban, 36% rural and it won't be long before Anchorage lays claim to half of the state's population.

Today, the greater Anchorage metropolitan area has more than 290,000 residents. Founded in 1914 as the chief construction camp when the Alaska Railroad was building track to Fairbanks, Anchorage is a major port. Prince William Sound provides shelter from winter storms and high winds despite tidal differentials that can be as much as 40 feet between low tide and high tide.

Fairbanks, with 60,000 people, is a very distant second. It is also the site of the main campus of the University of Alaska, and its newspaper, the Fairbanks *News-Miner*, has a long history as one of the state's best newspapers read by all the political cognoscenti. This is due in part to the fact that one of the reporter/editors, Bob Bartlett, became first, one of the non-voting delegates to Congress, and, following statehood, was elected as one of Alaska's first United States senators. Later, the paper's publisher, Bill Sneddon, became good friends with Senator Ted Stevens and in his will left a large, expensive yacht to Stevens, who, facing some challenging financial needs at that time, sold it right away.

Despite its proximity to the North Slope and Prudhoe Bay, Fairbanks did not succeed in cornering the majority of the pipeline supply business. Though the distance to Anchorage was greater, the North Slope oil producers concluded it was the better headquarters site.

Fairbanks' major disadvantages included the long, well-below-freezing winter nights which can last 20 hours. Often, a pea-soup fog settles in for weeks at a time. To say the least, the incidence of depression, over-consumption of alcohol and spousal abuse is higher in Fairbanks than most other places in Alaska.

Many Alaskans, as well as many Americans, buy into the myth that Alaska was called "Seward's Folly" when the United States purchased the 375 million acres in 1867 for a mere $7.2 million. For almost a hundred years, virtually all Americans furthermore believed that Alaska was primarily nothing but ice and snow inhabited by Eskimos. All these perceptions were wrong. The "Seward's Folly" phrase was coined 20 years after the fact, and even in the 1860s there was recognition on the part of some that Seward had committed "grand larceny" on a scale not seen since President Thomas Jefferson and his Secretary of State, James Madison, negotiated a comparable scale "theft" from France by obtaining France's Louisiana Territory for $15 million.

Some newspapers looked down the road and speculated "there's gold in them thar hills." Those capable of looking over the horizon or those with a nose for a good bargain were complimentary of Seward's Alaskan purchase. Thaddeus Stevens, the conservative "avenging angel" and no friend of Seward's, said the purchase of Alaska would be Seward's greatest legacy.

Those who could not look over the horizon questioned Alaska's lack of infrastructure and the daunting task of trying to create one. Of course, "fiscal hawks" in Congress doubted there would ever be a decent return on the investment.

The supporters turned out correct, for there *was* gold in the hills, and the Klondike Gold Rush of 1897 was one of the largest America has ever seen. Later, "liquid gold," oil, was discovered, first at what would become the Naval Petroleum Reserve #4, and then in 1968, at Prudhoe Bay.

By the early 1900s hundreds of gyppo miners, as well as some professionally trained geologists, were scattered all over Alaska, hiking up mountain draws and following rivers to their origins, staking claims under the generous provisions of the 1872 Mining Law, which literally gave away the hidden mineral wealth lying both on the surface and under the surface for a minimal investment to prove up the claim.

Congress, however, made a major mistake: The United States did not "own" the land, and thus it was not theirs to give away. Alaska's original inhabitants, native tribes like the Tlingit and the

Haida, as well as the variant Eskimo bands, were the rightful and legal owners.

Congress, in approving the appropriation for the purchase, failed to address the issue of extinguishing Native claims, leaving a cloud over every mineral and homestead filing; over time this unresolved issue festered.

These matters never crossed Congress' mind, despite having recently gone through a civil war which turned in part on the subject of human rights. Congress viewed Native Americans, however, as sub-humans, not granted citizenship and voting rights until 1923.

The unaddressed issues would linger for more than a century before being resolved by a series of status changes. In a sense, each settlement in the series was necessary before the next could be dealt with.

First, early on, the federal government opted to have Alaska run by the U.S. Army as a military department. In one of those little ironies of history the colonel assigned to be the department commander was named Jefferson Davis (no relation to the president of the Confederacy). He took charge the day following the Russian hand-over on October 17, 1867.

The Army ran Alaska for the next ten years, but in 1877 the U.S. Treasury Department became federal administrator. That experiment was short-lived, lasting but two years before Treasury turned it back over to be run by the military again. This time, however, the United States Navy represented federal ownership for the next five years.

On May 17, 1884 Alaska was redesignated as a Federal District and the chief administrator was a governor appointed directly by the president. The only remaining federal district today is the District of Columbia, our nation's capital, Washington, D.C.

In 1913, Alaska again received new status, formally becoming a territory with the governor again being a direct appointee of the president.

These governors were often from "outside" as well as friends or hefty contributors to presidential coffers. Sometimes a president might ask for a recommendation from his Interior secretary, but not often. Being from the outside they were viewed with suspicion by the local citizens of Juneau, the capital, which is isolated from the main part of the state, in southeast Alaska. Unfortunately, these territorial governors rarely realized the incredible amount of annual rain that falls on Juneau, which sees only a handful of blue-sky days with little wind and warm sun.

One of the Alaska Territory's longest serving governors was a newspaper editor from Massachusetts, Ernest Gruening. Appointed by Franklin Roosevelt in 1939, he served 14 years, until 1953. He remained popular enough that five years later, in November of 1958, he was elected along with Bob Bartlett to represent Alaska in the United States Senate. Like Bartlett, he also served ten years before being upset in the Democratic primary in 1968.

Alaska's territorial status lasted until it became the Union's 49th state on January 3, 1959.

Statehood created additional pressure because, as with all the other changes in status, it did not extinguish Native claims. The Statehood Act promised the state the right to choose 103 million acres from the federally owned lands for sustaining long-term economic development. It was no surprise then that Alaska began a process of identifying lands thought to be high in mineral value, or, as in the southeast, heavily timbered. The state felt its land selections should come before the Natives made their selections. Land lawyers told the state to guess again, that the Native claims had to be addressed first.

The first "building block" was passage of the Alaska Statehood Act in the fall of 1958. Sentiment in Alaska in support of statehood had been slowly building for a number of years, but the biggest obstacle was President Dwight D. Eisenhower, who doubted that Alaska had the infrastructure in place to conduct business and commerce without still needing a heavy federal subsidy. Of course he was correct, but in politics, goals, desires and wishes often trump reality.

Additionally, partisan politics played a role with some fearing that Alaska would always send Democrats to Congress. The decision to also admit Hawaii offset that fear because it was thought that Hawaii would always send Republicans. Such predictions would bring an ironic smile to present-day politicians.

The Statehood Act dodged the issue of Native land claims, leaving it to later resolution. The Act had granted the state the right to select for its purposes 102,350,000 million acres as well as also granting the state the most generous mineral leasing revenue formula – 90 percent – of any state admitted to the Union. Other western states had been granted just 37.5 percent of the mineral leasing revenue.

The second major building block was the imposition of a "land freeze" in late 1966 by Interior Secretary Stewart Udall. He ordered the suspension of all land conversion programs pending settlement of Native claims. At that time the state had only selected 25 percent of its land allotment.

The third building block was the discovery of oil at Prudhoe Bay in 1968. This made securing a route for a pipeline an imperative and attorneys for the oil companies quickly recognized Native claims had to be settled.

The fourth building block was passage of the Alaska Native Claims Settlement Act in December of 1971. This act granted Natives the first right to select their 44 million acres, but the acreage in large part had to be in reasonable proximity to Native villages. It also set up 13 Native Regional Corporations to manage Native resources and assets including an outright grant to the Natives of $900 million from the U.S. Treasury.

The fifth building block was passage of the Trans-Alaska Pipeline Act in December of 1973, made possible by the settlement of the Native Claims Settlement Act. The key to passage of the pipeline authorization though was section 17-d-2 of the Settlement Act which authorized the Interior Secretary to withdraw from the public domain at least 80 million acres of "national interest conservation" lands and study them for possible redesignation as national parks, wildlife refuges, national monuments or forest service wildernesses and/or wild and scenic rivers.

These five elements culminated in eventual passage of the Alaska National Interest Land Claims Act in late 1980 and the signing into law of the act on December 2, 1980.

At the outset of World War II, the then-territory was home to only 72,000 people. Its strategic location led to the Pentagon sending 152,000 troops there. These troops were kept busy building military complexes and air bases: Fort Richardson, Fort Wainwright, Fort Greely, and the air bases at Elmendorf and Eilson. In addition, with Canadian assistance, the ALCAN Highway was quickly built, which would result in further migration to Alaska.

A little known facet of the war effort in Alaska was the formation of a group of American women who served as ferry pilots, flying planes built by the United States but given to the Russians to help their fight on the eastern front. These women pilots ferried hundreds of planes from a base outside of Great Falls, Montana to Fairbanks where the planes were turned over to Russian pilots.

Many of these troops fell in love with the country, much as Wallace McGregor did. They returned after the war, often with their new brides.

Some of the war veterans who returned headed for the isolation of the back country to try their hand at trapping or gyppo mining. A few survived and thrived; many more lasted little more than one winter. Some disappeared altogether. Ironically, many of these free souls developed intense hostility for the federal government. It was a love/hate relationship that persists to this day.

Because of its remoteness and vastness, Alaska has long relied on federal largess, especially when it came to developing infrastructure; ironically, Alaska gets far more from the nation's treasury than it pays in taxes, with the annual expenditure of federal dollars for Alaska consistently topping $10 billion.

What McGregor and many of the "Cheechakos (A common term long-time Alaskans use to reference newcomers from the Lower 48 or the outside) turned natives" from the south did not recognize was that since the beginning of the 20th century there was intense interest in the eastern United States by the so-called "effete elite" in seeing the "whole untrammeled" swath of ecosystems in Alaska preserved for posterity, not exploited for their potential resource conversion. Conflict between developers/boomers and preservationist/conservationists began brewing and erupted into a full-fledged fight in the 1960s and 70s.

These winds of change would cause no end of stress and angst for McGregor, his partners and other Alaska in-holders who at the end of 1980 found themselves surrounded by millions of acres of newly designated federal lands. These new set-asides seemed to many Alaskans (who already had little use for the federal government) to come with too much regulation and too little common sense.

The list of eastern "effete elites" started with one of President Jimmy Carter's predecessors, President Theodore Roosevelt. Though he never actually set foot in Alaska, TR's footprint on the early history of conservation in Alaska is large and indelible.

*Theodore Roosevelt*

Early in his life, TR developed an interest in ornithology which, coupled with his voracious reading, led him to some of the early conservation writers, especially those writing about conservation in Alaska. Among these early writers were Dr. C. Hart Merriam, chief of the U.S. Biological Survey, and William H. Dall, a paleontologist with the U.S. Geological Survey. As TR read these and others, like Sierra Club founder John Muir, he became, even while still governor of New York, an ardent "environmentalist" in every sense of that word.

Once he succeeded to the presidency in 1901, he had the world's best "bully pulpit" to preach the gospel of conservation and preservation, and that he did. Helping TR immensely in selling the need to provide government protection of Alaska's "crown jewels" were the incredible photos of Seattle photographer Edward Curtis. His black and white photo portraits captured for many Alaska's beauty and vastness, and remain impressive to all privileged to view them today.

Curtis' nickname was "shadow catcher" and he is the subject of a fine biography by former *New York Times* reporter and columnist, Tim Egan, who grew up and attended school in Spokane, Washington.

Curtis' mantle of great photography from Alaska was assumed by Ansel Adams, who also worked in black and white. Many of Adams' fine photos were skillfully utilized by the Sierra Club, the Wilderness Society and other conservation groups which came together as the Alaska Coalition. This diverse group of folks, in Alaska as well as across the nation, dedicated themselves to obtaining the set-asides of scenic natural habitats promised in ANCSA. Not before or since have the major conservation groups united around one issue and one goal like they did on the Alaska lands legislation.

Just as the advocates for protecting entire ecosystems in Alaska began working together over 100 years ago, so did the opponents – the economic boomers: developers, timber barons, canneries and miners.

TR was well aware there were numerous "bonanza seekers" who wished to exploit all of Alaska's natural resources for their own selfish ends. These original boomers saw Alaska as theirs for the taking, but TR knew, particularly when the Antiquities Act was passed by Congress in 1907, that he had the tools to thwart the exploiters, which he proceeded to do.

Already aware that overfishing was occurring in areas along Alaska's coast, TR easily envisioned the over-mining and deforestation that could occur if large corporations were able to secure land which he believed belonged to all citizens. Instinctively, TR also knew one should think large when it came to providing protections.

He laid the groundwork and set the scene when he culminated his "great loop" trip around the west in the spring of 1903 with a rousing call to arms before a large audience in Seattle, in the name of saving Alaska.

Speaking to the Arctic Brotherhood, TR knew he would receive a mixed welcome for membership of the group was predominately made up of folks who made a living being the jumping off point for shipping goods and materials to Alaska. Pounding the pulpit, he gave a rousing defense of his aggressive protection policies.

Even before his speech in Seattle in 1903, TR had begun a series of executive proclamations setting aside areas in Alaska for preservation in their natural state. On August 20, 1902, he declared the 300-mile-long group of forested islands known as the Alexander Archipelago a federal reserve and off limits to any development or resource extraction. On that day 4.5 million acres off the coast of southeast Alaska were protected in perpetuity.

*Gifford Pinchot*

With the help of his talented friend, Gifford Pinchot, who was his first chief of the USDA Forest Service, and later a governor of Pennsylvania, Roosevelt followed this up with an executive order creating the 4.9 million-acre Chugach National Forest near Anchorage. It encompassed much of the Kenai Peninsula, Prince William Sound and the Copper River delta.

Later, in 1907, he placed almost all of southeast Alaska into the 6.9 million-acre Tongass National Forest. His keen interest in birds led to his creating numerous bird sanctuaries throughout Alaska, the

largest of which today is the 16 million-acre Yukon Delta
National Wildlife Refuge.

*William Howard Taft*

Many presidential historians today believe the primary reason
TR broke with his chosen successor, William Howard Taft, and
challenged him in the 1912 presidential election, was Taft's abject
failure to follow up on and support TR's conservation policies.
Taft quickly became a tool of big business interests and TR never
forgave him for it.

TR had his own coterie of big business supporters, but unlike
most on Wall Street, these were supportive of conservation and
had personal wealth that enabled them to travel, explore and write
about their experiences in Alaska. Pinchot was among this group,
but perhaps the most noted was E.H. Harriman, one of the
wealthiest men in America.

Harriman was chairman of the board of Union Pacific, father
of Averill Harriman, who founded the world renowned Sun Valley
Resort. A state park is named after him in eastern Idaho.

Harriman became an ardent supporter of conservation and
today is more noted for a journal he kept of his hunting trips in
and around Alaska, viewed as an important authoritative account
of the flora and fauna, than for any lasting accomplishment
attached to his wealth.

Other writers, adventurers, and artists weighed in during the
ensuing years. Charles Sheldon, clearly a member of the "effete
elite," kept extensive journals while on various hunting trips

throughout Alaska. His books as well as his memoirs were read by many of the eastern establishment for, like Harriman, he was independently wealthy and retired at age 35. His passion became an intense drive to protect the area in and around what today is known as Denali National Park.

On February 26, 1917, his efforts culminated in success when President Wilson signed legislation creating Mount McKinley National Park.

Some of these early advocates, like TR and Charles Jackson, were inspired by the writings of John Muir, who wrote eloquently about his trips in 1879 and 1880 up Alaska's Inside Passage. Another early book that inspired the conservation movement was William T. Hornaday's precedent-setting *Our Vanishing Wildlife*.

Bob Marshall, for whom a Montana wilderness area was named, attracted further attention to Alaska with his memoir of life in the outback, entitled *Arctic Village*, which came out in 1933. A co-founder of the Wilderness Society, he would spend days hiking and backpacking by himself exploring many of the hidden valleys in the Brooks Range. Today, Marshall is viewed by many as the inspiration for and thus the progenitor of the massive Gates of the Arctic National Park.

Artist and author Rockwell Kent lived with his son on an isolated island off the Alaska coast for a couple of years. His book, *Wilderness*, published in 1920, has been likened to Henry David Thoreau's classic *Walden*.

The now legendary author of *A Sand County Almanac*, Aldo Leopold, was another co-founder of the Wilderness Society who promoted Alaska protection, as was the great and long-serving Supreme Court Justice William O. Douglas. His spouse, Kathy, a talented attorney in her own right, carried on the work by joining various Alaska Coalition lobbying forays up to Capitol Hill.

Standing like King Canute swinging his sword at the incoming and rising tide of conservation and environmentalism were boomers like Governor Walter J. Hickel, who served as President Richard Nixon's first Secretary of the Interior, and the nation's 38th Interior chief. Hickel was aided, abetted and supported by Anchorage *Times* publisher Robert Atwood, and other "chamber of commerce" types who felt Alaska was so vast that there was no way puny humans could ever mar, scar or damage it.

These boomer mentalities never saw the oncoming train called the Alaska Coalition, which rolled right over them. Nor did they have any awareness of the exploitive schemes that plagued Alaska in the 1910s and 1920s.

Wallace McGregor once told me in an interview that had he known more about the Wrangell-St. Elias area's history, he might have thought twice about exploring in the area. Only in his "golden years" did he learn more about the history and the dark cloud that hung over the gorgeous mountains that constitute so much of the Wrangell-St. Elias National Park.

Anyone digging into that early history would be appalled at the level of greed and graft that existed. A student of history would discover that valuable coal leases were simply given away to cronies of the 24th Interior secretary, former Seattle Mayor Richard Ballinger. These giveaways lay at the heart of a long and bitter dispute between Pinchot and Ballinger during the two years (1909 to 1911) that Ballinger served in President William Howard Taft's cabinet.

Ballinger was a true free-market, pro-business Republican. Taft chose him to replace TR's last Interior secretary, James R. Garfield (son of the former president). Pinchot's suspicions that Ballinger was going through a sham process in giving away these valuable coal leases in the Wrangell-St. Elias Mountains was quietly investigated and thoroughly documented by an Interior department investigator, Louis Glavis.

Glavis' investigation revealed Ballinger's role in facilitating sale of these leases to two of the Gilded Era's wealthiest individuals: J.P. Morgan and Samuel Guggenheim. The two were referred to by some critics as "Morganheim."

Others simply referred to the pair as the "Alaska Syndicate."

*Richard Ballinger*

Historian Douglas Brinkley, a noted author and history professor at Rice University, tells this story in his fine book, *The Quiet World,* one volume in a three-volume history of various Alaska land issues. The books document Alaska land ownership and the problems therein, from the time of the 1867 purchase from Russia to the ultimate disposition of the complicated, varied land issues and the set of compromises that created the Alaska Native Claims Settlement Act in 1971 and the passage of ANILCA in 1980.

In his book, Brinkley states that Pinchot firmly believed, "Ballinger was offering sweetheart deals to railroads, mining outfits, and cattle concerns and logging conglomerates on public lands. Ballinger insisted that the U.S. Land Office (forerunner to the Bureau of Land Management) had only one job: to let private concerns divvy up the public domain in an orderly manner."

While a Senate committee investigation subsequently and questionably exonerated Ballinger of wrong-doing, tough questioning by committee counsel and future U.S. Supreme Court Justice Louis Brandeis thoroughly exposed Ballinger's anti-conservation views which led to his resignation in March of 1911.

Though always acting in support of Alaska boomers, former governor and Interior secretary Walter J. Hickel thought of himself as a conservationist.

He even published under his name a book written by a ghost-writer that sounded some progressive and conservation views. Called *Who Owns America*, it sold modestly well for awhile. No reputable Alaskan or nationally known conservationist, however, would step forward to validate Hickel's self-serving claim. Being fired by President Richard Nixon for questioning the president's Viet Nam war policies, on the other hand, made Hickel a bit of a hero briefly to the anti-war movement.

A few months after Idaho governor Cecil Andrus became Interior secretary in early 1977, he traveled to Anchorage to attend a Western Governor's Association meeting. While there, he met with Hickel, who had returned to private life. He asked Andrus to drop by for a courtesy call at his suite on the top floor of his hotel, the Captain Cook.

While there, Hickel made a comment to Andrus that should resonate with all Alaskan citizens:

"Mr. Secretary," he said, "Could I ask a favor of you? When you next come to visit Alaska, would you come in the dead of winter? That way you'll really get a better picture of what Alaskans have to contend with nine to ten months of the year. Don't be like others who come just in the summertime with its long days. That's not reality."

# 3

# Oil politics

*Man standing next to the trans-Alaska pipeline.*

There's an old political cliché that most folks associate with the Watergate scandal: "Follow the money."

In Alaska, the statement should be amended to, "Follow the oil."

When the oil began to flow through the recently completed trans-Alaska pipeline on June 20, 1977, that's exactly what Alaskans did.

Oil was the new crowned king and has pretty much remained the dominant element in Alaska's political and business life ever since.

Over the last 50 years oil has driven Alaskan politics more than any other industry in the state's history. Through taxes and fees levied by the state, it has contributed billions to the Alaskan economy and billions to the Alaska State Treasury.

There also is the Permanent Fund (more on this later), a product of, and a tribute to, the genius of Governor Jay Hammond, who spearheaded an effort that placed on the Alaska ballot a requirement for a certain amount of the oil revenue to be sequestered away into a savings fund. From the interest off that fund there would be an annual distribution to legal residents of Alaska based on the number of years they had lived there. The principal was to remain forever sacrosanct. It was overwhelmingly endorsed by the people of Alaska and over the years has placed billions into the pockets of Alaskans.

One has to wonder just where the state would be today if the liquid gold had not been discovered.

When ARCO hit the jackpot by drilling a producing well, it set off the kind of frenzy that hadn't been seen in Alaska since the early gold rush days. People in the city of Fairbanks, in particular, smelled the roses of seduction and started making grandiose plans to be the lead jumping off point for supplying those constructing the pipeline and those building the oil industry complex at Prudhoe Bay.

Over 1,200 companies registered to do business in Alaska or bid on the state's first lease sale, on September 10, 1969, which brought into the state coffers almost a billion dollars. Alaskan legislators began discussing other ways to tax and/or access this revenue stream with additional severance taxes topping the list.

The oil industry flooded Juneau with lobbyists and lawyers, all charged to minimize the bite out of their corporate earnings that the legislature seemed to be planning. The industry tolerates some taxes but when in their opinion things start to look too confiscatory, they draw the line. Much of the impetus for more and higher taxation stemmed from wild guesses regarding the reserve size.

Estimates of the size of the reserve varied widely but eventually the number 9.6 billion barrels seemed to become the accepted figure.

The major oil companies initially made many mistakes, but they did get one thing correct: They were going nowhere without a comprehensive resolution to the various native land claims which at that time were still being ignored. Without a resolution they knew there would always be an unacceptable cloud on their title.

Almost three years after the discovery of the Prudhoe Bay oil field, the major oil companies helped drive an apparently successful settlement, the Alaska Native Claims Settlement Act (ANCSA) with Alaska's natives and Eskimos that obtained most of the Natives' major goals: more than 40 million acres of land primarily selected from lands adjacent to their villages; over $900 million in direct payments; the formation of 13 Native-run regional corporations and a royalty on future mineral revenues that gave them a stake in the state's economic future.

Despite appearances, the bill did not settle everything. Mary Clay Berry in her book (*The Alaska Pipeline: The Politics of Oil and Native Land Claims*) quotes then-Idaho Republican Senator Len B. Jordan stating at an informal Senate hearing on proposed amendments to ANCSA only 90 days old, "That isn't much of a bill we wrote." Montana colleague, Democratic Senator Lee Metcalf, reportedly whispered back, "That was a lawsuit we wrote."

Compounding the native claims process was the fact that Congress, in the process of making Alaska the 49th state in late 1958, had settled on a large grant of land to the state to assist Alaska in achieving its economic independence. The state was granted 103 million acres of federal lands – an unprecedented grant to any new state in the history of the nation.

While many Alaskans felt the state ought to be able to be first in line, Alaska's natives felt their selections should be first. While this issue was being debated the Department of the Interior, under Interior Secretary Stewart Udall, instituted in 1967 a land freeze that stopped all forms of federal withdrawals so as to preserve the status quo. The move was decidedly unpopular with most Alaskans.

The Statehood Admission Act also granted the state an unprecedented share of mineral lease proceeds generated off of federal lands. Most western states received 37.5 percent, the federal government received 10 percent and the remaining 52.5 percent would go to a federal irrigation and land reclamation fund. Alaska, however, was to receive 90 per cent.

Indeed, if there was one interest group in Alaska other than oil that seemed to fare well through out the entire process, it was the Alaska mining industry. Well organized and well led, it was able to protect, and in fact enhance, its presence and its rights. Their lobbyists in both Juneau and D.C. were tough, effective advocates.

The fight was on.

It was in this period that the fight over Alaska entered my life.

On January 1, 1971, I began work in Washington, D.C., for a small independent news bureau owned and operated by A. Robert Smith. Smith was the long-time D.C. correspondent for a string of Oregon newspapers including the *Oregonian*, the *Eugene Register-Guard*, the *Medford Mail Tribune*, the *Salem Statesman* and Bud Forrester's papers in Pendleton and Astoria. From time to time he also, on a "spot news" basis, was retained by *The Lewiston Morning Tribune*. Smith is the author of several fine books including the definitive biography of Wayne Morse (*Tiger in the Senate*), the iconoclastic United States senator from Oregon noted for switching parties and, along with Alaska Senator Ernest Gruening, one of the only two Senate votes against President

Lyndon Johnson's request for passage of the Tonkin Gulf Resolution.

Smith recruited me away from the *Spokane Chronicle* in December of 1970 to join his news bureau and take the lead responsibility for covering what went on in D.C. for the *Anchorage Daily News*, the *Ketchikan Daily News* and the *Sitka Sentinel*.

I jumped at the chance to go to Washington, D.C., at the age of 23 to be a reporter on the scene, and was especially fascinated by what was happening in Alaska at the time.

Working for Bob and Kay Fanning, who then owned the Anchorage morning newspaper, and for Lew Williams who owned the papers in Ketchikan and Sitka, was also pleasant because they recognized how much of Alaska's future was being determined in the halls of Congress. Almost all my copy was banner headlines in those papers.

The *Anchorage Daily News*, the morning newspaper, ran a distant second to the *Anchorage Times*, the afternoon newspaper, in circulation. Its owner, Bob Atwood, was considered to be one of the most influential people in the state. He was extremely involved in Republican politics and enjoyed unparalleled access to the governor's office and the congressional offices. Having chaired the Alaska Statehood Commission, he considered himself to literally be the "father of Alaska."

Atwood had retained the Griffiin/Larabbee News Bureau to cover D.C. for his paper a couple of years before I arrived. Up to that point Mary Clay Berry, who had been assigned to the beat, had no real competition. We enjoyed a friendly rivalry.

Because of the importance of resolving the native land claims issue the political environment I walked into in January of 1971 was charged and electric, and the congressional delegation involved in it was one of the most colorful in the nation.

I first met 38-year-old Nick Begich, who had won the seat in the November 1970, election. The congressman-at-large was an ambitious school guidance counselor, teacher and for eight years (1962-1970) a state senator in the Alaska Legislature. He won the Congressional seat by defeating the winner of the Republican primary, future U.S. Senator and Alaska governor Frank Murkowski, in the 1970 election.

Begich was a family man who with his wife, Pegge, had six children. The oldest, Mark, later became a mayor of Anchorage before being elected to the U.S. Senate in 2008. The son was then narrowly defeated for re-election in 2014 by the Republican candidate, Dan Sullivan, despite having earned high marks for his job performance. His handicap was he was a Democrat.

*Nick Begich. Photo by U.S. House of Representatives.*

The elder Begich, the congressman, was born in Minnesota in 1932. Both his parents had immigrated to America from Croatia. He appeared to be on his way to an academic or teaching career when he and his young family moved to Alaska in the late 1950s. From teaching he turned to being a guidance counselor, and at the time of his election to the state senate in 1962 was serving as the superintendent of the Fort Richardson schools. The "political bug" bit Begich hard and few were surprised when he went for a seat in the state senate, and won. He surprised some observers again when, eight years later, he won Alaska's sole congressional seat.

Begich came across as a man on the move even in a world like D.C. where most everyone seems to be on the make. Even to a greenhorn reporter like myself, it did appear he first analyzed everything he voted on in terms of whether it would help or hinder his plans to challenge in the 1974 Democratic Senate primary the incumbent, Senator Mike Gravel. Not surprisingly,

Gravel did not trust Begich and there was little contact between the offices.

Begich, while in the Alaska legislature, had a reputation for being a hothead, temperamental and disrespectful to his seniors. Someone (probably Ted Stevens) took him aside and explained that kind of behavior might go unpunished in Juneau, but it wouldn't fly in D.C. Begich did a complete reversal, showing great deference to his seniors, especially the thin-skinned chair of the House Interior committee, Representative Wayne Aspinall from Colorado. Begich was almost too obsequious.

Begich and his legislative aide, Guy Martin, carefully mapped out where they thought every member of Congress was on their issues, and whether Begich had courted them and/or knew them. Those Begich did not know he would take time to sit close to on the House floor and make their acquaintance.

Every few weeks, Martin would organize an information "dump" of some sort and would blanket all the other members' offices with information about some aspect of Alaska and its economy. Begich did all of this without ever expressing any personal animosity towards those that might disagree.

He even won grudging compliments from his various adversaries.

Besides Begich, the key players in the House side of the debate on the Alaskan lands issue included Representative Morris Udall, D-Arizona and Representative John Seiberling, D-Ohio. Other House members playing important roles were Representative Sid Yates, D-Illinois; Representative John Saylor, D-Pennsylvania; Representative Norm Dicks, D-Washington; Representative Lloyd Meeds, D-Washington; and, the future House speaker, Tom Foley, D-Washington.

Begich, however, will most be remembered as the congressman who disappeared in a plane with Majority Leader Hale Boggs from Louisiana. Boggs was campaigning with Begich and making appearances at several fundraisers for Begich. On October 16, 1972, flying in a Cessna 310 between Juneau and Anchorage, their plane disappeared without a trace. To this day it remains a mystery.

Begich's disappearance occurred just three weeks before the election. This was too short a time period to produce a certificate declaring him dead and the seat vacant. Alaska law required he remain on the ballot. Thus, State Senator Don Young, the Republican nominee from Fort Yukon, was defeated in November by a deceased incumbent, losing by a 44% to 56% margin. Ironically, this first defeat was the only congressional race Young ever lost; as of this writing he is the longest serving Republican member of the House, having been in Congress for 42 years so far.

Young went on to win the special election in March of 1973, defeating Democrat Emil Notti, 51% to 49%. Notti was one of the leaders of the Alaska Federation of Natives and its first president. His near election was the closest any Native candidate was to come to being elected to a major office in Alaska until Byron Mallott won the office of Lt. Governor in 2014.

*Don Young*

While Young has held Alaska's at-large seat ever since, periodically he has had close races. His closest call came in a tight primary race in 2008 against Lt. Governor Sean Parnell, who came within 305 votes of defeating Young. Parnell went on to inherit the governor's office when Sarah Palin resigned in July of 2009. He then won a full term in 2010 but his bid to win a second full term in 2014 was thwarted when independent Bill Walker, a popular former mayor of Valdez, and Byron Mallott, the Democratic candidate for governor, formed an independent ticket with Mallott taking the second spot. They succeeded in narrowly beating Parnell and no doubt their independent ticket was aided by the support of former Governor Palin. She eschewed her former number two because in her view and that of many Alaskans, Parnell had cozied up too close to the oil and gas industry by supporting additional tax relief for them.

Young, on the other hand, has always credited his early success at holding the seat to his strong support for the trans-Alaska pipeline, about which Begich was initially ambivalent.

Young is a unique character in and of himself. He sometimes has struck people as bufoonish, but he's also a genuine Alaskan original – by occupation a trapper, a riverboat captain, a teacher – and he's smart like a fox. Few would have dreamed he would become the longest serving Republican of the House, which he became with the start of the 2015 Congressional session.

As he grew in seniority, like Ted Stevens, he became more and more skilled at the appropriations game.

His name became synonymous with earmarks, single issue items attached to must pass bills with no relation to the context of the bill It reached the point where he successfully had an earmark of $110 million literally for a much-discussed bridge to nowhere. Supposedly built to someday connect with a road from an island airport to the nearby community, it stands as a monument to power and seniority in the House.

He also knew how to delay legislation by offering amendment after amendment to bills such as the Alaska Native Claims legislation and later to the Alaska National Interest lands legislation.

There's a roguish charm about him, though, that makes it hard to dislike him. He has a great sense of humor and clearly enjoys the life of a congressman.

Young and Andrus would josh around with each other, call each other names, the way Andrus would also josh around with Wyoming Senator Alan Simpson.

Andrus told one interviewer a few years after the d-2 debate that Young loved to call him names. He once told Andrus that he'd love to get him up to Fairbanks and "By God, Cece, there won't be enough left of you for dog meat!" To which Andrus replied, "I'll be in Fairbanks and by God, we'll see!" Of course when Andrus stayed in Fairbanks during the d-2 media tour, he was treated cordially and with respect. No one threatened him or yelled at him.

Alaska's junior senator in 1971, Democrat Mike Gravel (gruh-vel), was a completely different story.

Born in Massachusetts, he entered the Army after high school. Upon receiving his honorable discharge, he attended and graduated with a degree in General Studies from Columbia. He headed for Alaska with the clear intention of running for public office. His narrative was that he first drove cabs in Anchorage before getting into the real estate business.

He enjoyed enough success to be able to take the time to run for a seat in 1963 in the Alaska House and win. Two years later he stunned the state by winning the speaker's seat amid charges that he had lied to several folks and the incumbent speaker charged that Gravel had double-crossed him. This reputation would dog him throughout his public career.

In 1966, Mike Gravel sensed the vulnerability of incumbent Senator Ernest Gruening. Emphasizing his youth and energy, he spent months visiting various Native villages and the smaller communities across the state.

Following a carefully prepared campaign game plan, with just a few weeks before the 1968 primary, he unleashed the first total television saturation campaign the state had ever seen. It included a half hour biographical piece that showed over and over on all the state's TV stations as well as a deluge of ads. It worked. Gravel upset Gruening in the August primary.

A key aspect of Gravel's "bush" strategy was capitalizing on Alaska Native anger with the aging incumbent for his less than strong support for their land claims. The early time he had spent in flying to most all of the Native settlements around the state paid real dividends. With one-sixth of the population and a tendency to vote as a bloc, it was a smart move on Gravel's part.

*Ernest Gruening*

Many Alaskans were either employed directly by the military or were economic beneficiaries of the military presence. Thus, Gruening's vote against President Lyndon Johnson's Tonkin Gulf Resolution, which gave him the "authority" to wage war against the North Vietnamese, was not a popular move.

Today, Gruening, and Oregon Senator Wayne Morse are revered by folks in the Peace Movement and descendants of Vietnam anti-war protests. At the time, though, it clearly was a major contributing factor to Gruening's defeat.

Gruening contributed, however, by not taking the Gravel challenge seriously until it was too late.

In 1966, Gravel had hired Joseph Napolitano, the first of the many masterful "political consultants" who came into vogue in the 60s and multiplied in D.C. like rabbits. They plotted the blitzkrieg media campaign that overwhelmed Gruening.

*Mike Gravel*

Gruening did not know what hit him nor did he take his defeat lying down. The 81-year old former territorial governor of Alaska mounted a write-in campaign as an independent, but it was too little too late. In November, Gravel won the seat with 45% to Republican banker Elmer Rasmuson's 37% and Greuning's 18%.

In one of those ironic twists of fate, Ted Stevens, who had narrowly lost the GOP primary to Rasmuson in August, became Alaska's senior senator when on December 24, 1968, Governor Walter J. Hickel appointed Stevens to replace Alaska's other original U.S. senator, Bob Bartlett.

Appointing Stevens was the smartest thing Hickel ever did for the people of Alaska. Essentially, he also went back on his word, having promised Carl Brady, one of his oldest friends and strongest supporters, the first vacancy that occurred in the delegation. Brady had also been a major fund-raiser for Hickel.

In later years, Hickel said the first person to weigh in for Stevens was none other than President-elect Richard Nixon, who Hickel bumped into at a reception at D.C.'s venerable Shoreham Hotel on December 11 just after he received word of Bartlett's death of a heart attack in Cleveland. Hickel was in D.C. at the request of the Nixon transition team because Nixon was planning on naming some of his cabinet choices the next day, including that of Hickel as Interior secretary.

Hickel quickly walked over to the President-elect to give him the news and Nixon immediately mentioned he knew Ted Stevens. According to Hickel, Nixon first asked him what he was going to do. Hickel said there would be three people on his short list: Elmer Rasmuson, the banker who had beaten Stevens in the August Republican primary; Hickel's long-time good friend, Carl Brady, and Stevens. Nixon volunteered that he'd met Ted and then point blank asked Hickel if he had the courage to appoint Stevens. Nixon in effect was telling Hickel he couldn't go wrong by naming Stevens. Hickel ultimately took the unsolicited advice, but not before having both Brady and Stevens come by his

Anchorage home for a visit in which Brady graciously let Hickel off the hook by voluntarily stepping aside.

Hickel announced his selection of Stevens on December 23, which was 10 days before Gravel was to take office. Stevens, who went on to serve longer than any other Republican ever served in the U.S. Senate, was the senior senator, and Gravel the junior.

As I did my daily walk through the offices of all three members of the delegation, Gravel was the least available and the most distant. He left it to his chief of staff, Joe Rothstein, to talk to me. Stevens and Begich, on the other hand, always insisted on seeing me every day when I came by.

Stevens was notorious for having a trigger temper and more than once he would charge out of his inner office and lay into me for not getting a story quite right or quoting him exactly. He paid very close attention to how he was portrayed in every newspaper. Unlike Gravel, he had folks in his state offices clipping announcements of baby births, weddings and graduations. A new Alaskan mother, for example, would receive a package with a book courtesy of the Library of Congress on the ins and outs of motherhood along with a congratulatory note from the senator. He mined agencies throughout government that might have surplus books or brochures on subjects he thought might be of interest to his constituents and literally inundated Alaskans. Gravel had nothing like it.

Gravel did have stars in his eyes. One could see Gravel thought destiny had greater things in store for him. Two incidents stand out from the two years I covered Alaskan affairs.

The first was Gravel's obtaining in mid-1971 from some source the so-called "Pentagon Papers," classified documents detailing the many failings of America's Vietnam War policies. Gravel spent hours reading these into the Congressional record, breaking down several times and crying. He received lots of national publicity but it is debatable how much good it did his national image or his image in Alaska.

The second incident, in August of 1972, had to be one of the more embarrassing moments for the citizens of any state in the annals of political history. It came at the Democratic National Convention at Miami Beach on the sultry, humid August night that

South Dakota's George McGovern was to accept his party's nomination for president and deliver his acceptance speech.

One of the many "seconding" the nomination speeches was an Alaskan native female who was a friend of Senator Gravel's. Instead of delivering her one minute remarks, she yielded her spot and the convention microphone to Senator Gravel who had suddenly strode onto the platform. Much to the consternation of Senator McGovern and his campaign manager, Gary Hart, Gravel stunned the convention by nominating himself to be the vice presidential running mate on the ticket. He demanded that the McGovern forces open up the nomination for vice president to the entire convention. Gravel's plea to be nominated to be McGovern's running mate fell on deaf ears, but his antics caused convention proceedings to be delayed by several hours, enough so that when McGovern rose to give his acceptance speech it was well past prime time all across America. Neither McGovern nor Hart ever forgave Gravel and for many Alaskans it was one embarrassment too many. One could mark Gravel's decline from that point on.

Earlier that year, Gravel also ostensibly had written his political manifesto, *Citizen Power*, the near traditional book that many presidential wanna-be's use as a pretext to travel the country before formally declaring their candidacy. Not surprisingly, the banal reworking of various speeches by Gravel was universally panned.

The irony is that McGovern's selections left people scratching their heads almost as much as they would have had McGovern acquiesced.

When Gravel sought re-election in 1974, two things saved him. First, as noted earlier, at a crucial point in the 1973 debate over whether to authorize the trans-Alaska pipeline, Gravel for once worked with Stevens and the newly elected Congressman-at-large, Don Young. Gravel authored an amendment that immunized the proposed pipeline from further legal challenges for any reason which led to construction (read lots of jobs) getting underway almost immediately. To his credit, Gravel carefully navigated the amendment through the Senate and when it came up for a vote on July 17, 1973, the measure was deadlocked in a 49-49 tie vote. Vice President Spiro Agnew dramatically cast the tie-breaking vote and work on the pipeline soon started. Gravel demonstrated that he could, on rare occasions, be a workhorse, not a show horse. He could also be a team player, if he so desired.

The other break Gravel received was that the GOP nominated State Senator C.R. Lewis, a national officer of the John Birch Society, to be Gravel's opponent. As conservative and as libertarian as most Alaskans are, the state's voters just could not put a John Bircher in the Senate. While Gravel's support was waning considerably, he rolled over Lewis, 58% to 42%.

Unfortunately, he read this as a mandate to continue his mercurial ways.

The most fascinating member of the delegation, and the one I came to know best, was the temperamental – some would say feisty, ornery and volatile – Ted Stevens.


Born in Indianapolis in 1923, he was 48 years old when we first met. Little did I realize then he would go on to be the longest serving Republican senator in American history until finally defeated in 2008 at the age of 85 by Anchorage Mayor Mark Begich, the eldest son of the former congressman.

Many observers believe Stevens would have won even that race had he not been subjected to a charge from the Justice department for accepting gifts from friends and interest groups for questionable favorable votes on matters of their interest. It was later revealed, after the election, that the prosecution willfully withheld a key piece of evidence from Stevens' defense counsel.

A judge reprimanded the Justice Department for this egregious breach and the charges against Stevens were dropped. This of course happened after the election Stevens narrowly lost.

*Ted Stevens. Photo office of Senator Stevens.*

Stevens's story of his up-by-the-bootstraps upbringing by several relatives, from Indiana to California, is a remarkable tale of diligence and perseverance overcoming all odds. There are some fascinating contradictions in his life today compared to his early years. For example, he had on display in his office a surf board. Try to relate the image of a serious, somber, sober, often humorless senator with that of a 19-year-old surfer boy riding the waves off of Santa Monica. Imagine some surfing song by the Beach Boys playing in the background. Then picture the young Ted Stevens on the surf board! It's hard to imagine.

That Alaskans kept returning Stevens to the Senate should not surprise either, for as he grew in seniority his power and ability to bring home the bacon played a crucial role in helping Alaska and Alaskans develop the infrastructure necessary to build a diverse economy in the 21st century. Over the years, Stevens directed billions of federal dollars to his adopted state.

It can safely be said, and has been noted elsewhere many times, no other senator in American history has ever had so central a place in his state's public and economic life for so long a period of time. A few senators, like the long-serving Robert Byrd of West Virginia and Warren Magnuson from Washington state, might approach Steven's level, but "Uncle Ted," as he was affectionately called by Alaskans, was truly in a class by himself.

His delivering the goods began in earnest when he, along with Gravel, delivered the legislation that allowed construction to proceed on the trans-Alaska pipeline, which cost several billion dollars to build. It stretched 900 miles, from Alaska's North Slope and Prudhoe Bay, where oil was discovered in 1968, to the ice free port of Valdez on the southern coast.

Stevens's considerable accomplishments are best left for a solid biographer to recount. As one who covered him closely for two years, though, I knew he was a hard worker. Unfortunately, he was hard on his staff – a demanding perfectionist with a tart tongue and a sharp mind; he went through several chiefs of staff during those two years.

One, George Bullock, originally from Portland (and a member of the national champion American Legion baseball team that had Mickey Lolich as its star pitcher), attended Stanford. Bullock was teaching at the University of Alaska-Fairbanks and doing political analysis for the local TV station when Stevens spotted him and wooed him away to D.C.

Unfortunately, I inadvertently contributed to Bullock leaving the senator's employ all too soon. Bullock allowed me to quote him on the record that Stevens might be reconsidering his heretofore hawkish stance on the Vietnam War. Stevens exploded when he read it and read Bullock the riot act. Bullock wouldn't back down since Stevens had indeed speculated aloud to his staff chief that he might be changing into a more dovish stance. They parted company, but fortunately we remained friends.

Beneath Stevens' gruff exterior there was of course a tender-hearted individual deeply devoted to his wife and his children. I'll always remember sitting on the inside steps of his home in Virginia at a Christmas party he held for his staff and a few friends. We just casually chatted about things in general. No one could doubt his deep devotion to improving the welfare of his Alaskan constituents.

Despite his chewing through chiefs-of-staff, for many years his executive secretary, Celia Niemi, stood and stayed loyally by his side.

Stevens had worked in the Department of the Interior for several years before returning to Alaska to be the U.S. Attorney for Alaska. At the end of the Eisenhower Administration he was the solicitor for the Interior Department working closely with then Interior Secretary

Fred Seaton. Thus, he knew much about the workings of the most important department in the government for Alaska.

Stevens also had a way of cultivating his senior colleagues including those across the aisle. He slyly ingratiated himself to West Virginia's long-time senator and Majority Leader Robert Byrd, often giving the Democrat a needed vote on a critical issue.

The upshot was that by the time Cecil Andrus became Interior Secretary in January of 1977, Byrd, too busy with his Majority Leader duties, let Stevens "chair" the Interior Appropriations subcommittee. That's correct: though it was a Democratic-run Senate and a Democratic White House, Andrus and his department answered to a Republican chairman.

Fortunately for the Interior department during Andrus' tenure, on the House side the chair was a superb Democratic congressman from Illinois, Sid Yates. He and his chief of staff, Mary Bain, did a fine job of protecting Andrus during the four years we had to answer to Stevens with regard to the department's budget on the Senate side.

Two of Alaska's early governors played key roles in the ultimate passage of the d-2 lands legislation, also: Former Valdez mayor William A. "Bill" Egan, Alaska's first governor and its fourth governor, Bristol Bay fisherman, bush pilot and guide Jay Hammond.

Egan served from the beginning of statehood on January 3, 1959 to 1966 and again from 1970 to 1974. He was succeeded by Hammond, who served from 1974 to 1982. The two men are easily the most popular governors ever to serve Alaskans.

Egan was instrumental in helping to get the trans-Alaska pipeline bill passed and signed into law in 1973 by President Richard Nixon. Hammond was a critical behind the scenes negotiator with Andrus on the final boundaries of the ANILCA bill.

A former Stevens' staffer, Jack Quisenberry, who ran the senator's Juneau office, told two brief stories revealing Egan's popularity.

*Bill Egan*

When Egan returned to Juneau to begin his third term there was a bit of a parade from the Juneau Airport into the Capital City. Quisenberry was inside a store as Egan's entourage drove by. One elderly woman, after watching the governor, rushed back into the store and with tears in her eyes, exclaimed to all within hearing, "Bill Egan is back! Bill Egan has returned. Thank God, Bill Egan is back!"

The second story was a description of one of the best, brief 15-second television commercials ever run by any campaign. The ad opened with a Native chief, with weather worn face, sitting on a stool in the studio as a spotlight turns on him. The chief turns and looks right into the camera. He asks a brief rhetorical question then answers it:

"Bill Egan? You don't have to tell me about Bill Egan. I know Bill Egan!"

That was it, and pure dynamite as it connected with Alaska voters, many of whom did indeed know Bill Egan.

Egan almost always made a point of dropping by to brief me on his meetings while in Washington. A gentleman, he spoke softly but was always prepared. He did have a nasty chain-smoking habit, and lung cancer finally killed him at the age of 69.

Egan knew oil was going to be a big part of Alaska's future, but it was his Republican successor, Jay Hammond, who is given the lion's share of credit for pushing through the Alaska legislature the idea of diverting a portion of the taxable revenue from the state's cut and placing it in a Permanent Investment Fund that would be invested conservatively.

Hammond insisted the proposal be placed on the general election ballot, knowing the legislature would be much less likely to tap into the fund for other purposes if the voters had publicly sanctioned that it be held sacrosanct. His real genius came through in the form not only of using (living off of) the interest on the fund and never touching the principal, but in providing every legal resident of Alaska an annual dividend check.

*Jay Hammond. Photo office of Governor Hammond.*

Distributed in early December, it fluctuates due to the price of oil, but the fund is worth billions and Alaskans can usually look forward to an annual payment between $1000 and $2000, much of which is plowed back into the local economy.

Of all the Alaskan governors involved in the debate about the future of Alaska and the Alaskan lands legislation, Andrus thought Jay Hammond understood the competing interests and did the best job of maintaining a delicate balancing act.

Andrus felt Hammond was a true conservationist, but had to be careful in how he dealt with the issue recognizing at the time almost 90 percent of Alaska voters were opposed to additional federal designations of parks, refuges and wilderness areas.

Hammond's book, *Tales of a Bush Rat Governor*, is one of the best political autobiographies written by any governor in recent times.

## GOVERNORS OF ALASKA

1   William Allen Egan (D) 1959-66
2   Wally Hickel (R) 1966-69
3   Keith Miller (R) 1969-70
4   William Allen Egan (D) 1970-74
5   Jay Hammond ( R) 1974-82
6   Bill Sheffield (D) 1982-86
7   Steve Cowper (D) 1986-90
8   Wally Hickel (Alaska Independence/R) 1990-94
9   Tony Knowles (D) 1994-2002
10  Frank Murkowski (R) 2002-06
11  Sarah Palin (R) 2006-09
12  Sean Parnell (R ) 2009-14
13  Bill Walker (I) 2014-

Governors Egan and Hammond, as well as Senator Stevens and Congressmen Begich and Young had a special appreciation for some of the many factors that make life in Alaska so much different from the Lower 48. A huge part of their mission in representing their state was educating other members about these differences.

For example, there are very few roads and highways outside of the greater Anchorage area. The primary mode of transportation is by air, often in small bush planes – supercharged tail-dragging Cessna 180s and 185s, Cessna 310s, Beavers, Otters, Grumman Gooses, Aero Commanders, and 80-year-old Douglas DC-3s. Alaska, not surprisingly, has the highest loss of life per air miles traveled in the United States.

Thus, well-equipped airfields with radar and navigation lights are a much higher priority than are roads. Many Alaskans like it this way and they look to their members of congress to provide satellite coverage for telecommunications. Senator Stevens was a huge supporter of public television and public radio in Alaska because he knew the private sector outside of Anchorage would always feel there were not enough numbers to justify investment.

Thus, there are numerous villages throughout Alaska that are truly isolated, and the primary mode of transportation is boats in the summer and snowmobiles in the winter.

Most Alaskans, whether Natives or not, believe they have a constitutional right to hunt and fish where they please, when they please. They term it "subsistence hunting and fishing." Alaska Fish and Game does set seasons and takes, but poaching is commonplace far from authority.

In the early months Andrus was at Interior, he was almost suckered by a member of the National Park Service's Alaska team into proclaiming that there would be *no* hunting in the new national parks being contemplated in the d-2 legislation. After all, hunting was banned in national parks in the Lower 48.

Fortunately, the error was caught and excised from the text before Andrus delivered the speech. He and others then pondered the matter. Native and non-Native subsistence hunting is viewed in much of Alaska as an absolute right.

A compromise of sorts was soon fashioned which allowed for the continuation of subsistence hunting in the new national parks, but no sport hunting. Drafts of the Lands Claims Act started appearing which referenced areas adjacent to and some even within park boundaries to be called park preserves, if the hunting was particularly good in the area.

These often reflected the migratory routes of some species. In other areas, such as McGregor's Orange Hill site, the park preserve designation was adopted because of the numerous dall sheep in and around Orange Hill. Many a plane flew in with hunters who then headed for the hills to try for a trophy to take home. Of course Natives and non-Natives could still hunt in the preserves also.

One very distinctive feature regarding subsistence hunting is that it is not defined as merely a Native right; it also can apply to packers and hunters who have utilized subsistence hunting over the years to supplement their other food.

Even Alaska's constitution mentions the right to subsistence hunt and makes it clear it is not just a Native right. One can see, though, how this can lead to abuses.

Alaska also is far from being a homogeneous culture. Both the Native population and the Caucasian population have had to work at transcending differences and suspicions. Those who can walk and work successfully with both cultures are often viewed with suspicion by both.

Andrus once mentioned that he really wished most of the d-2 land could have been protected as U.S. Forest Service wilderness but that the idea wasn't going to fly in D.C. given the politics in both the nation's capital and in Alaska. Some latter-day commentators believe he is correct. They base their view on the belief that the Forest Service would have spent far less money in managing the park, staffing up and signage than the National Park service.

A friend, Alaskan reporter Craig Medred, once wrote me, "Wilderness in Alaska doesn't need to be managed (despite the millions the park service has spent writing management plans and "patrolling" the backcountry). All it needs is to be protected from roads. And Alaskans, for reasons varied and complicated, have proven themselves extremely good at that over the last 40 years. Maybe too good."

Medred went on to point out a few of the inconsistencies that mark the political scene.

He said most Alaskans would probably be happy now to join in screwing anyone out of anything connected to a mine. Alaska is a different place, some of it much better, some far worse. Tightly controlled mining is now frowned upon; out-of-control four-wheeler access ripping up the backcountry? Yee-haw! Let's go.

Some tourist on the Kenai River taking home a legally taken cooler of red salmon? Way bad.

Dead zones around villages from unregulated hunting; serious overfishing of Chinook in the name of subsistence? Well, you know they need their subsistence . . .

He concluded, "I had great hopes after the D2 debate ended that this state might be able to move forward toward some sort of sensible, sustainable, forward-looking economy. I think I might have been wrong."

# 4

# People, debate, passage

*Secretary Andrus looks at a grizzly bear in the distance from an observation point within Denali National Park during the week-long tour of proposed d-2 lands in July of 1978 he led for national media journalists. Behind him from the left is Gerry Lubenow from Newsweek's San Francisco bureau; Cynthia Wilson, the executive director of the Interior Department's Alaska Lands Task Force; Joe Hildreth, the Alaska State trooper Governor Hammond insisted accompany the Secretary. To the far right is Joel Connelly, political columnist for the Seattle P-I. Photo courtesy National Park Service.*

When Cecil Andrus left Plains, Georgia, as Interior Secretary-designate in late November of 1976, on the plane ride home he took out his lined yellow pad to write down the list of priorities for the department he and President-elect Jimmy Carter had discussed. Number one on the list was fulfillment of the d-2 Alaska lands set asides for new national parks, wildlife refuges, wilderness areas, national monuments, and wild and scenic rivers.

As was his habit, though, Andrus did not just write down "Alaska lands legislation." He began developing a strategy and a game plan both from the internal agency standpoint as well as the external political world. He knew it would neither be easy nor simple, that powerful economic forces would line up against it. On the other hand, he knew the president had entrusted him with an enormous responsibility – to deliver on the promise candidate Carter had given the conservation community and to gain passage of what would become recognized as the single greatest conservation bill in the history of the nation.

Andrus, consistently backed by the President, would prove to be up to the challenge.

Early on Andrus penned these words to a friend in the conservation community:

"Now, as Secretary of the Interior, I will have the chance to influence actively the greatest national park opportunity in history. After many years of study and effort, we have reached the decision point on the "D2" Alaskan lands set asides proposal.

"The breadth, the grandeur and the intensity of the Alaskan scene match our every hope. Outstanding parks must be established, preserving entire ecosystems on a scale to meet the requirements of the most renowned wildlife display in the Western Hemisphere. We must act in such a way, however, that Alaska's original native people have a realistic chance to retain their richly unique culture. And both goals can be met in harmony with intelligent and careful economic progress for the state of Alaska.

"Over the past decade a great effort has been made to develop but still protect, to plan yet control Alaska's future for maximum long term benefit. Despite its youthful strength, and boisterous energy, remarkable new standards of cooperative private and governmental planning have been set in Alaska. The credit goes to many, from the native groups who forced the issue of lands claims settlement, to the citizens and government leaders who listened and helped. I commend particularly the thoughtful vision and conservation achievements of Governor Jay Hammond.

"It will not be easy, but there is still room for Alaska to retain and even enrich its diversity. Opportunities exist concurrently for social and economic growth, as well as for native cultural integrity, wildlife refuges, wilderness and great national parks."

Anyone who knows Andrus recognizes this longer description of the basic formula that has guided him well in his public sector career: "First, you have to make a living; then, you have to have a living that is worthwhile."

The passage and signing into law of Public Law 96-487, was the fulfillment of section 17-d-2 contained in the 1971 Alaska Native Claims Act. Often, when talking about the Alaska lands issue, those most familiar with it would just refer to the issue as the "d-2 lands" debate.

Just who was the genius and just how did the section come to be in the bill?

Most of those intimately involved in the Alaska lands legislation credit David Hickok, a resource specialist with the Federal Field Committee that had a charge in the late 60s and the 70s to review all federal lands in Alaska for recommendations for highest and best uses. Hickok was visiting Washington, D.C. in the spring of 1970. In a meeting with Bill VanNess, counsel to the Interior committee and a long-time friend and supporter of the committee's chair, Washington state U.S. Senator Henry M. Jackson, Hickok mentioned the thought to VanNess, who immediately liked the idea, drew up the simple language and inserted it.

According to Robert Cahn, a veteran writer for the *Christian Science Monitor*, in a long article published in the *Audubon Magazine* in the early 80s, several other key supporters who had worked with and around the Federal Field Committee had also discussed the Land Claims settlement act becoming a vehicle for some new national parks and wildlife refuges in Alaska.

These folks included some early conservation group leaders such as Ted Swem, George Marshall and Stewart Brandborg of the Wilderness Society, Ed Wayburn of the Sierra Club, and Joe Fitzgerald of the Federal Field Committee. All agree, however, that it was Hickok who broached the subject with VanNess, who then inserted the language.

Initially, the simple provision said the Secretary of the Interior, "is directed to review all public lands in Alaska and within three years recommend to the Congress areas appropriate for inclusion in the National Park System and the National Wildlife Refuge system." Eventually later amendments extended the deadline for seven years to December 18, 1978, and indicated the Interior secretary was expected to recommend at least 80 million acres to fulfill the intent of the provision.

It took some conservation groups and their leaders a while to recognize what was in the claims settlement act when signed in December of 1971 by President Nixon. Once they focused on it, however, they recognized a once in a lifetime opportunity to plan and protect some entire ecosystems, and they had a chance "to do it right the first time."

Folks within the Interior department, though, moved more quickly, particularly those within the National Park Service and the Fish & Wildlife Service. Both organizations realized they could come close to doubling in size the acreage they could manage for posterity through good conservation practices.

Former Park Service Director George Hartzog mobilized his organization rapidly and he himself conducted Nevada Senator Alan Bible on a wonderful tour of the possible set-asides in the summer of 1971. Bible chaired the Interior subcommittee for Parks and Recreation. This adroit move by Hartzog quickly won a solid ally for the cause.

Andrus had a set of eight to ten advisors on the Alaskan lands issue who formed a true inner circle.

There were two that were "first among equals:" The assistant secretary for Land & Water, attorney Guy Martin, who, despite being a Democrat, had accepted an offer from Jay Hammond to work for him as his commissioner of the Department of Natural Resources. As the Assistant Secretary for Land & Water at Interior, he played a key role in working with the other "first among equals," Cynthia Wilson, the Secretary's Alaska Lands Working Group leader.

A former assistant to Lady Bird Johnson and Elizabeth Carpenter and a former lobbyist for the National Audubon Society, Wilson came to Interior having worked on several Alaskan issues while with the National Audubon D.C. office. She also participated in the early meetings which led to the formation of the Alaska Coalition. In 1976 she flew to Alaska and then over-flew or visited all of the d-2 proposed land withdrawals for redesignation as part of the four great protection systems.

*Guy Martin. Photo courtesy Martin Family Collection.*

Martin had one distinct advantage over others in the inner circle of Andrus advisors: he had actually lived and worked in Alaska. As such, he had first-hand knowledge of the preceding legislation that had to come before Section 17-d-2 could be fulfilled – from the Statehood Act to the Native Claims Settlement Act to the Trans-Alaska Pipeline Act. Besides being the legislative director for Alaska Congressman Nick Begich when the Native Claims Settlement Act was passed, Martin set up and ran the first Alaska State Office in D.C. for Governor Bill Egan.

Thus Martin was a key player when the Trans-Alaska Pipeline Act was passed.

A third key assistant secretary who always came to the meetings well prepared and was no shrinking violet when it came to advocating for his bureaus was Bob Herbst, the assistant secretary for fish, wildlife and parks.

Martin's successor in the Alaska state office was the extraordinarily capable John Katz, who ran the office so well and in such a bi-partisan, non-partisan manner that he remained in the post through the terms of the next eight Alaskan governors. Katz worked closely with the congressional delegation as well, and he was especially adept at reading Senator Stevens. Folks at Interior and within the Alaska Coalition considered Katz to be the most effective opponent of their goals, in part because he was always calm, deliberate and never got personal.

While serving as Governor Jay Hammond's original Commissioner of Natural Resources, Martin was intimately involved in the state's land selections and establishing the TAPS right-of-way so that pipeline construction could commence and oil could start flowing south from the North Slope.

Martin sacrificed more than most. Before joining Interior and working with Andrus, Martin had what looked to be a bright political future in Alaska.

Intimately familiar with all the major as well as minor resource issues there, he was viewed as a comer. It is fair to say that in coming to D.C. to work for Andrus and the Carter Administration, Martin forsook a promising political career in his home state. He seems not to have regretted the choice he made.

If Andrus was Carter's quarterback, then Cynthia Wilson was his "quarterback coach." She kept day to day overview on everything that had anything to do with Alaska. Both she and Martin played the key roles for Andrus and his Department of the Interior, with most of its numerous agencies and bureaus fully engaged in working for passage of the d-2 legislation.

*Cynthia Wilson*

They were capably supported by Gary Catron's Congressional and Legislative Affairs office, which worked closely with the White House's legal and legislative team led by Frank Moore and deputy Jim Free. Andrus was not particularly a fan of Free, who felt everything and anything having to do with Alaska had to come across his desk. Free was smart enough, though, not to challenge Andrus directly. Instead, he had minions in the White House nipping at just about everything else Andrus might be doing.

"The last best chance to do it right the first time," which became the mantra of the conservation and environmental groups across the nation supporting the pro-D-2 lands debate, achieved something for the first and only time in the history of the nation's environmental community: The campaign to protect entire ecosystems in Alaska united every single environmental and conservation group. It hasn't happened since. (See appendix for list of the 55 members of the Alaska Coalition).

In 1976 the leadership of most of the major environmental organizations met in Washington, D.C., and yes, some of the organizing meetings took place in the board room of the National Rifle Association. Initially the NRA supported the concept of the Alaska lands legislation because many of its members are hunters and sportsmen. Additionally, they wanted to show solidarity with the National Wildlife Federation. They soon reversed themselves.

The passage of the Alaska Native Claims Settlement Act had given the environmental community the opportunity to demand extensive additions to the four systems as the price for their acquiescence to the Claims Act and their caving in on the TAPS pipeline project after some symbolic posturing in opposition.

Two items guided their thinking.

Though they fought hard against the legislation immunizing the pipeline and its sponsors from further legal or legislative delays, they recognized the probability that they would lose on the floor of the Senate.

The second point was their keen awareness of a new tool unwittingly being handed them by the Nixon Administration – a little bill authored largely by Washington state's junior senator, Henry "Scoop" Jackson, entitled the National Environmental Policy Act which gave birth to the requirement to conduct an environmental assessment or a full-fledged Environmental Impact Statement if any activity involved federal funds or agencies.

Armed with these tools and a unity of purpose seldom seen, the leaders of the Wilderness Society, the Sierra Club, Friends of the Earth, the National Wildlife Federation, the Audubon Society, the NRDC, the Alaska Conservation Association and others organized into a galvanizing unit that proved to be invaluable in obtaining passage of the Alaska lands bill.

James Turner, author of *The Promise of Wilderness*, put it this way:

"The campaign for Alaska became a focal point of American environmental politics in the late 1970s. With the Sierra Club in the lead, the environmental community organized under the banner of the Alaska Coalition – which emerged as a well-oiled advocacy machine, spanning dozens of national organizations and 1,500 local and national affiliates; its cogs and gears linked to the nation's environmental constituency with a professional lobbying campaign in Washington, D.C."

*Brock Evans*

The leadership for the effort, of necessity, was three individuals with considerable lobbying experience in D.C.

Two of the three had been top lobbyists and staff for the Sierra Club. The third, Doug Scott, started out with The Wilderness Society. Though vastly different in temperament and style, the combination was effective. Chuck Clusen was selected to be "the Supreme Allied commander," and proved to be equal to the task. His two top lieutenant/lobbyists were Brock Evans and Doug Scott. Altogether, the Sierra Club "loaned" outright, in addition to "sub-contractors" they continued to pay, some 50 folks in all.

Those three, Clusen, Evans and Scott, along with Andrus, could be characterized as the "Four Horsemen of the Alaskan Lands." If one can visualize Andrus as the quarterback, and continue the football analogy, Chuck Clusen, the chairman of the Coalition, would be the slotback, the one who could run, or catch a pass, and inspire his team with focus and discipline. Brock Evans would be the halfback, the one who could block for the quarterback if he was running or passing and could in turn run himself for valuable yardage. The fullback, the three yards and a cloud of dust would be Doug Scott, the lead day-to-day lobbyist who performed magnificently in just grinding out.

*Doug Scott*

While formally an advocacy group capable of receiving donations because of its non-profit status, the Coalition's budget was largely a myth created at the beginning of each year. All three candidly admitted in interviews an enormous debt of gratitude to Laurence Rockefeller, Jr., who underwrote many of their activities or saw to it that one of the sponsoring groups picked up the check.

*Chuck Clusen*

During the course of the pivotal year, 1980, the Alaska Coalition did a mailing to a million conservation households, several times sent out alert telegrams to 100,000 key supporters and opinion leaders and took out full page ads in the nation's major dailies. These ads were not only financed by Rockefeller, they often were written by him.

If there was one "outside" interest group that rendered indispensable service and support, it was the Alaska Coalition. Their key core team played an outstanding role both nationally in rallying support within Congress, and in Alaska, where they were a truly besieged minority but nonetheless stood fast. Folks like Jack Hession and Stan Senner, in addition to Clusen, Evans and Scott are but a few who come to mind. Key congressional staff like Rep. Morris Udall's Mark Trautwein, as well as Rep. John Seiberling's aide, Andy Wiessner, also played critical roles.

*(The appendix contains a list of many of those who can claim parenthood, but it also likely left some key players out either because I did not know nor had I read of their involvement. To those I failed to mention, my apologies.)*

In Alaska, the brave and hearty souls who stood up for the legislation were few and far between – but they stood out for their courage in defying the boomer mentality then dominating Alaskan thinking. Folks like Celia Hunter, Bob Weiden, David Quice, and Gordon Light deserve their own chapters in any new version of *Profiles in Courage*.

Two early leaders of the effort to protect as much of Alaska as possible were Stewart Brandborg of the Wilderness Society and Tom Kimball, from the National Wildlife Federation. The Wilderness Society became part of the Alaska Coalition. The NWF did not formally, but Kimball did much behind the scenes in the early days. The NWF's primary official concern was monitoring language that would in anyway restrict hunting.

For this very reason the National Rifle Association also belonged to the Alaska Coalition, but soon dropped out.

*Gary Catron (left). Photo by the National Park Service.*

Andrus knew how important the Alaska Coalition lobbyists and D.C. representatives were, so he often talked to their leadership personally following negotiation sessions which they could not attend in person. Likewise, he often offered advice and counsel to Clusen, who had deep respect for Andrus' political acumen and listened carefully.

As the point person for the Administration, the Secretary was often the target of comments and suggestions for items within the bill or tactics on how to get the bill passed. He developed a set of concentric circles of advisors with personal staff and key department personnel such as Solicitor Leo Krulitz, Assistant Secretaries Davenport, Herbst, Martin, and Larry Meierotto on the inner circle along with Under Secretary Jim Joseph and Cynthia Wilson. The next circle was largely the key folks in the White House led by deputy White House Counsel Jim Free, and the next circle were key members of the relevant committees on the Hill, and the final circle was comprised of the lobbyists and leadership of the Alaska Coalition.

Andrus was also well aware that as early as 1968 Alaska's Natives had become increasingly impatient with both the federal and state government. Some native leaders were even starting to suggest militancy and war against the white population. They wanted a large area around their villages so as to continue their subsistence hunting and fishing; they wanted a substantial cash payment, and they wanted regional native corporations set up, some 13 in all, with independent boards of directors and stocks (with dividends if a year was profitable).

These positions evolved over a period of almost ten years and who spoke for the Alaska Federation of Natives (AFN), the primary Native lobbying group, was sometimes hard to discern. One of the early galvanizing forces educating the Native community to the validation of those claims was the emergence of a Native newspaper, the *Tundra Times*. Edited by Eskimo Howard Rock and printed in Fairbanks, this weekly became the bible of the Native community's drive to get their rights recognized.

Anchorage attorney and former Alaska Federation of Natives General Counsel Don Craig Mitchell has written two fascinating and detailed books on the subject of Alaska Natives and their land claims (*Take My Land, Take My Life: the Story of the Alaska Native Claims Settlement Act*; and *Sold American: The Story of Alaska Natives and Their Land*).

The Native community also insisted their claims took precedence over the state's right to select the 103 million acres it had been granted the right to select in the statehood admission act. Compounding the situation was a total land freeze on any selections put in place by Interior Secretary Stewart Udall in 1968.

In 1968 both the Senate Interior and Insular Affairs committee and the House Interior Committee held hearings in Alaska taking testimony as to what Alaskans would like, and not like to see in an Alaska Native Claims Settlement Act. Many Alaskans recognized, as did the oil industry, that without clarifying legislation their economic progress could be held up for years. Though yet to create the Alyeska consortium that would ultimately represent their pooled interests, all the major oil producers and refiners were calling for passage.

Ten years later another set of hearings would play a pivotal role in galvanizing American public opinion in favor of the d-2 legislation that called for protecting at least 83 million acres of the federal domain as new additions to the national parks system and the fish & wildlife refuge system.

By 1978, the long-time crusty chair of the House Interior committee, Wayne Aspinall from Colorado, had been replaced by Arizona's Mo Udall, a liberal conservationist, who then selected Representative John Seiberling of Ohio to be the chair of a special subcommittee on the future of Alaska and other public land issues.

One of Udall's top aides, Harry Crandell, was detailed to help Seiberling. Alaska Coalition chair Chuck Clusen viewed Crandell as a mentor and in many respects the "Godfather" of the Alaskan lands legislation. The stroke of genius on their part was not only to hold hearings in Alaska but also to hold hearings in five major cities across the Lower 48: Seattle to Denver to Chicago to D.C to Atlanta. The 1978 hearings helped immensely in generating support for the d-2 lands set asides.

Andrus developed and maintained close relations with both Udall and Seiberling for the duration. As always, there are implied quid pro quos among these consummate political practitioners. Of course it was pure coincidence when Andrus in 1979 traveled to Akron, Ohio, to meet with Seiberling to tour the Cuyahoga River Recreation Area and discuss its possible conversion to one of the new Urban National Parks.

Likewise, it was pure coincidence that in 1979 Andrus flew to Tucson to tour with Udall the Central Arizona Project which brought Colorado River water all the way to Tucson. He then also addressed a gathering at the annual meeting of Western Water Commissioners. Pure coincidence.

A telling precursor of Native interest in these various federal land issues had been the 1968 hearings held by both houses of Congress. Many Natives attended and testified at the Senate hearing convened by Washington's junior senator, Henry M. Jackson, on February 8, 1968, in the main auditorium on the University of Alaska-Anchorage campus.

In 1968 Senator Lee Metcalf from Montana sat in the chairman's chair when Jackson could not attend at the last moment. The committee could not help being moved by much of the Native testimony, which was supportive of some sort of settlement, but several dissenting voices were heard. Metcalf's untimely death 10 years later was a tough blow to the Alaska Coalition which had been looking to him to be their champion in the Senate.

If early on there was one specific opposition group not just to the Alaskan lands legislation but even to settling with Alaska's natives, it was the Alaskan Mining Association and its chief spokesperson, George Moerlein. He testified, ominously, that neither the federal government nor the state government nor the people of Alaska owed one dime or one acre to Alaska's natives. He cited the Act of Cession which Congress passed in 1867 when it approved the ridiculously low price of $7.2 million for Alaska.

Out of such little things can large and wrong conclusions be drawn. Instead of being seen as part of their community and a colorful part at that, some folks began to see miners as the enemy, with cause.

The five-year period from 1966 to 1971 saw an ever increasing number of Alaska Natives, both tribal chiefs and tribal members, journey to Washington, D.C., to make the case for settling their historic claims.

Early leaders of the Alaska Federation of Natives led the first wave with Emil Notti, the first president, charting the path. Others soon followed like State Senator Willie Hensley from Kotzebue, and young Byron Mallott, who in 2015 was elected lieutenant governor of Alaska, the first Alaskan Native so honored. Later, when Don Wright became AFN president, he too was a frequent visitor to D.C.

Others included the articulate John Borbridge, from southeast Alaska's Tlingit-Haida Tribe, and William Paul, a member of the Tlingits whose son, Fred, was a leading attorney for the Natives during the debate over land claims, the trans-Alaska pipeline and the d-2 legislation. Joining Howard Rock in representing the

North Slope's scattered and diverse Eskimos were Eben Hopson and the militant Charlie Edwardsen.

All belonged to a band of brothers, if there ever was such a group, who worked tirelessly for their fellow Natives and for all of Alaska. All belong in an Alaskan Hall of Fame.

Their labors were rewarded on December 18, 1971, when the Alaska Natives right to their homeland was acknowledged by President Richard Nixon as he signed into law the Alaska Native Claims Settlement Act. The act reinforced the state's right to claim the 103 million acres, from Alaska's total of 375 million acres, promised in the Statehood Act, but it also contained the famous (or infamous) Section 17-d-2 that required up to 83 million acres be placed in one of the four great conservation/wilderness systems: national parks, national wildlife refuges, national monuments and national wilderness areas.

It also set a deadline for the 83 million acres to be designated by December 18, 1978.

Alaska's Natives were granted $900 million from the Treasury and 44 million acres.

As is often the case with Congress, nothing much happened until 1976 rolled around and recognition grew that the deadline was all too rapidly approaching. Another significant event occurred when Congress passed and President Ford signed into law in mid-October of 1976 the Federal Land Policy and Management Act. This organic act for BLM gave the Interior Secretary new and additional powers to execute additional land withdrawals and was within two years cited as one of the authorities for additional withdrawals in Alaska.

Another critical event generating serious momentum was the recognition by disparate environmental organizations that a unified effort had to be organized and a massive lobbying effort orchestrated to ensure that all Americans understood the stakes and their share of the Alaskan patrimony. This led to the Alaska Coalition being formed in November, 1976.

The formation of the Alaska Coalition was the *sine qua non* in achieving eventual success. All their lobbyists, especially Clusen, Evans and Scott, worked closely with the Carter White House as well as Andrus and his team at Interior. Most importantly, when the end game came around they proved themselves adept practitioners who were able to compromise in order to achieve an eventual bill.

Early on, the Alaska Coalition produced a draft bill, largely written by Clusen with ample assistance from Evans and Scott, and a little over a month later, in December, 1976, they presented it to Representative Udall, suggesting he introduce it as the legislative vehicle on the House side.

In January of 1977, as the new incoming chairman of the House Interior committee, Udall did introduce the Alaska Coalition's draft legislation that sought to protect over 100 million acres. Their draft legislation became the controversial H.R. 39.

During the spring and summer of 1977—still new to the job— Secretary Andrus asked Interior agencies to develop positions and recommendations for him to sift through prior to a fall hearing before Congress on the Alaska legislation. To assist him in preparing for these hearings and for becoming the lead department whose primary congressional goal for the coming fiscal year was to secure passage of a bill, Andrus put together the Alaska Lands Working Group headed by Cynthia Wilson.

Wilson was to report directly to him and all the bureaus and agencies who wanted to be part of the action also were directed to report on any Alaskan affairs to and through Wilson. She and Martin were also his day-to-day contacts with the White House team working on passage of the legislation.

The result of these departmental meetings and task force sessions was a set of recommendations for an Administration bill on Alaska. The bill differed from the Alaska Coalition's draft, H.B. 39, in several respects, not the least of which was a whittling down of the proposed land withdrawals for the four systems to 93 million acres and a reclassification of the Arctic range east of Prudhoe Bay as the Arctic National Wildlife Refuge.

The Arctic range is home to the world renowned Porcupine Caribou herd. The Interior department's proposed legislation classified part of the area as wilderness—forever to remain inviolate, meaning no exploratory drilling for hydrocarbons *ever*.

This brought a strong, heated objection from the Energy and Commerce departments as well as Office of Management and Budget (OMB). President Carter, however, backed Secretary Andrus and the Interior recommendation, following a stroll by Andrus over to the Oval Office for a short visit with the President.

There were just a handful of people who understood the deep bond between Andrus and Jimmy Carter.

Right after his election in November of 1976, Carter met with a group of CEOs and executive directors of the major environmental organizations. Carter asked them for a list of names and few had Andrus on their list. For many, Andrus was not "green enough." Doug Scott and Brock Evans, both of whom had been the Northwest director of public affairs for the Sierra Club at different times, had Hawaii Congresswoman Patsy Mink at the top of their list. While Andrus' stand against a molybdenum mine near Castle Peak in the White Clouds was commendable in their eyes, as was his call to reform the Mining Law of 1872, they simply believed one could not trust any western governor.

In particular, some felt Andrus was too soft on the timber industry, which with the likes of Boise Cascade, Potlatch Corporation and Plum Creek harvesting at a rate well beyond sustainable yield in Idaho, should, in their eyes have led to sharp criticism from him.

Few folks are aware also that following his infamous malaise speech in which the President asked for the resignations of all his cabinet officers, Carter called just two to tell them not to worry: Cyrus Vance and Cecil Andrus.

Secretary Andrus appeared before the House Interior Committee in September of 1977, and with the strong support from the Alaska Coalition, he laid out the administration's case even though it called for less acreage to be set aside than did the Coalition's preferred vehicle, H.R 39.

Those who testified in opposition to the administration's Alaska lands legislation included some of the nation's most powerful and influential corporations. Exxon, Anaconda Copper, U.S. Borax, Louisiana-Pacific, the National Rifle Association, U.S. Chamber of Commerce, National Manufacturer's Association, National Mining Association, Northwest Mining Association, Alaska Mining Association, the state of Alaska, the Alaska Federation of Natives, the Teamster's Union and Citizens for the Management of Alaska Lands.

No big surprise perhaps: The administration's bill also encountered strong opposition from the state of Alaska, of course, and even the Alaska Federation of Natives objected to some sections.

The state objected to quite a few features in the bill, but to many it looked like they and industry were trying hard to renege on the *quid pro quo* contained in the ANCSA bill that paved the way for the pipeline bill to pass. Now the state was backing away from section 17-d-2.

Thousands of Americans, however, in the Lower 48 *were* paying attention. These folks, motivated by a million-household direct mail piece put together as part of the Alaska Coalition's goal "to win big in the House," as well as phone banks and full page ads running in the *New York Times* and the *Washington Post*, inundated their congressional offices to make sure their congressman was not simply deferring to an Alaskan colleague.

The Alaska delegation, however, was less than cooperative. During the first four months of 1978, Congressman Don Young undertook a number of delaying tactics, offering substitute amendment after substitute amendment in a gargantuan effort to stall and hopefully kill the House bill, but all to no avail.

The House, after adopting key amendments requested by the Administration, passed with the full support of the Administration, the Udall/Seiberling bill on May 19, 1978. The vote was a slaughter of those opposed to keeping the promise of 17-d-2. The expanded version of H.R. 39 won, 277 to 31.

The action next shifted over to the U.S. Senate and the renamed Energy and Natural Resources committee, where the proposed Alaska lands legislation had little support. This was due largely to Senator Stevens's determination. Despite his hot temper, he had managed to cultivate friendships with most of the members, especially the chairman, Senator Henry Jackson of Washington.

During the summer of 1978, Andrus and the team devised a strategy aimed first at keeping the pressure on opponents to work for a compromise and passage of legislation. This was especially critical with the December 18, 1978, deadline rapidly approaching.

Sometime early in the fall of 1978 several individuals within the Department of the Interior became aware that Secretary Andrus had quietly raised with President Carter the possibility of utilizing his absolute, unqualified power contained in the Antiquities Act to declare qualifying federal lands as National Monuments in order to ensure protection in perpetuity. Andrus was distinctly aware that Senators Gravel and Stevens might be able to utilize Senate rules to block any Alaska lands legislation being passed before expiration of the deadline.

As an old poker player he knew one should always have an ace up his sleeve. In discussing what options the Administration would have Andrus brought up with his solicitor, Leo Krulitz, assistant secretary for Land & Water Guy Martin, and Cynthia Wilson the possibility of the president utilizing the Antiquities Act along with his new powers under the BLM Organic Act unilaterally to exercise their respective land withdrawal authorities. He did not reveal that he had already raised the prospect with President Carter while on their August fly fishing float trip down the Middle Fork of Idaho's Salmon River.

All recognized that there were various legal requirements that had to be in place to make such designations effective and bullet proof from any legal challenge. They quietly began taking care of the necessary steps.

*Alaska Coalition team meets with the Administration to plot strategy for passage of d-2 legislation. Photo courtesy personal collection of Chuck Clusen.*

In early October, the executive director of the Alaska Coalition, Chuck Clusen, reached the same conclusion on the necessity for a back-up strategy. He too quietly wrote and urged President Carter to be prepared to use his powers under the Antiquities Act to make protective withdrawals should no bill be passed or an extension of the deadline achieved. Clusen's memo, shared with no one else, certainly validated for President Carter the wisdom of Andrus' earlier discussion.

I – at that time communications director for Andrus at Interior – brought another element into consideration at this point. My deputy Harmon Kallman in late fall brought the Antiquities Act to my attention and described how its power had been used since 1907 by almost every president.

Andrus and I began discussing a strategy to make it easier for President Carter to use this unrestricted land withdrawal and redesignation power under the Antiquities Act. Both of us were convinced Senator Gravel would figure out how to throw a massive monkey wrench to stall if not outright kill passage of any lands bill. This fall-back strategy would force opponents to come back to the negotiating table, Andrus believed. Events proved him to be prophetic.

Later, after Carter and Andrus had exercised their combined authority, I was asked by Jody Powell and Patricia Bario in the President's Communications office to give them a short explanation of the action for use with inquiring media. The memo is among the Andrus papers being reviewed and categorized today at Boise State University, the designated repository for Andrus' papers both from his terms as governor and his term at Interior.

The two years I spent earlier working for the *Anchorage Daily News* provided me with a working knowledge of the players and the issues that were at times helpful to the secretary. For example, when we first arrived in D.C., I told him that within a short time we would be working more closely with the Republican senator, Ted Stevens, than the Democratic senator, Mike Gravel. He asked why I thought that.

I gave him two reasons: "First, Mike Gravel is going to look you in the eye and flat lie to you. Stevens, on the other hand, will fight you tooth and nail, but if he gives you his word, you can take it to the bank."

"Secondly, Stevens is the work horse; Gravel is the show horse."

Andrus replied, "In over 15 years in politics I've never had anyone look me direct in the eye and flat out lie to me!" My response was a short, "Well, get ready."

All of this came true. Two months into the job, I one day picked up the phone with Andrus on the other end. "You were correct, Chris. The s.o.b. has flat lied to me. We'll be working with Stevens, not Gravel."

That proved to be the case. The contrast between the two became even more pronounced in 1978 as summer spilled into fall and fall fell into early winter. Stevens participated in every mark-up session held by the Interior committee. He always came prepared and knew every clause in all the bills. Stevens was a wily, smart political practitioner who knew all the tricks.

But he kept his word. He knew what he wanted out of the d-2 debate, stayed focused on his goal, and patiently worked to gain it.

Gravel, on the other hand, seldom attended such working sessions. Instead, he laid back in the weeds waiting for an opportunity to grandstand and hopefully derail any sort of compromise bill. It was for this very reason that Andrus did not trust Gravel. Andrus knew he had to have in his back pocket a strategy ready to kick into place should Gravel try to blow things up. When it transpired, as we had guessed it would, Andrus and the Alaska Coalition leadership were ready.

Andrus' order to staff at Interior, to begin preparing a Supplemental EIS on the land withdrawals being contemplated for President Carter's signature, was completed rapidly and thoroughly. All the necessary paperwork was well put together and the legal groundwork put in place awaiting only the President's decision. The rapid response and quality work derived from the fact that agency subordinates had reached the same conclusion Andrus had, that the endgame would entail massive land withdrawals for placement in new as well as expanded existing national monuments.

They had reached this conclusion in June long before receiving the order from Andrus to begin. Thus, there were dozens of professional public servants within Interior who indeed were critical to the success of the outcome. They did their job above and beyond. Most will forever remain unacknowledged, but they know and hopefully their key part in this historic undertaking will forever be of comfort to them. The fact that the withdrawals withstood an immediate challenge by the state of Alaska speaks for itself.

The second element of the strategy was to build more public support across the nation for protecting the d-2 lands. The Alaska Coalition had its fine, multi-faceted, multi-media strategy well underway, but Andrus knew the Department had to step forward and pursue the goal more aggressively.

Andrus ordered the public affairs office to put together a 7- to 10-day "educational" tour of the proposed d-2 lands with 10 to 15 key members of the nation's media so they could see for themselves what the stakes were in Alaska. He naturally expected that once educated they would in turn seek to educate their audiences – and did they ever.

The tour was a smashing success, in part because the group had great weather until near the end of the trip. In addition, the group that assembled to accompany the secretary was comprised of first-rate reporters who knew how to ask good questions. For example, Bill Keller was sent by the *Oregonian*. Keller later became the managing editor of the *New York Times*. *Newsweek* sent Gerry Lubenow from their San Francisco bureau. The *Seattle P-I* sent Joel Connelly, their ace political columnist and the alpha-wolf of the Washington state press corps. The *Anchorage Daily News* sent Tom Brown, a future managing editor, and the *Southeast Alaska Empire* out of Juneau sent Craig Medred. Several of these reporters were covering for chains. Thus, the reach of their stories and reports was extensive.

It was one of about only three times Andrus used his cabinet access to the Executive jet fleet available at Andrews Air Force Base, just outside of D.C.

Besides me, the secretary's entourage included Gary Catron, the Department of the Interior's assistant to the secretary and director of the office of congressional and legislative affairs (and a former aide to Idaho Senator Len B. Jordan), and Cynthia Wilson, the Alaska Lands Working Group head.

We made two refueling stops in the SAM Jetstar, one in Winnipeg, Manitoba, and the other at Fort Nelson in the far isolated northeast corner of British Columbia. I must admit there is something almost intoxicating about scooting along at 35,000 feet in a private jet. One really does get seduced by that insane sense of superiority and it's the exceptional person who can step off a private jet without feeling like a big shot.

It had to be something like that which led me to make an error of hubris which made me the subject of the news, instead of making sure my boss got all the ink.

I had carefully constructed an itinerary that reflected an effort to anticipate as many contingencies as a reasonable person would expect. There were infinite details as well as the preferences of the particular media to be contended with. I knew one major mistake could turn success into disaster, so I carefully constructed an itinerary that gave every reporter face time with the Secretary.

In addition, I made sure every reporter was with the Secretary in his plane on at least one leg of the trip.

Knowing that generating lots of publicity was the key to achieving the trip's objective, Andrus decided we would hold a press availability shortly after landing. We were then scheduled to meet with the Alaska Federation of Natives leadership, knowing they were the ones who still held some key cards critical to eventual success.

Andrus held his first press availability at the airport right after we'd touched down. With malice aforethought I had deliberately *not* invited the *Anchorage Times* to the availability or on the trip, figuring they would make a big deal out of sanctimoniously declining complete with a self-righteous "we can't be bought" editorial.

Tell them, however, that they weren't invited because of the clear bias they displayed on the news pages, and that was a whole different issue. Now they were a victim of an arbitrary, discriminating press secretary. Thus, they had a reporter at the press conference ask Andrus why they hadn't been invited.

Andrus of course said "Ask Chris." I gave a short, flip answer: "I thought I'd let Mr. Atwood know we can play hardball, too." This prompted several more questions aimed at me which my boss peremptorily cut off with a classic, wry look on his face as he curtly said, "Chris can hold his own press conference after mine."

Sure enough, the next day my front page story was as big as the Secretary's, much to my chagrin. However, with two hours until "wheels up" at 9 a.m. on July 6, I called the managing editor of the *Times* and explained we'd had a last second cancellation, that there was now a seat available and I was offering it to them first if they could get their reporter there in an hour. "We'll have our guy there in 45 minutes, and thanks," he said and hung up.

I lost a little skin off my nose but to this day I'm convinced if I'd handled it any differently, the *Times* would never have covered the trip. Since they now had to justify their presence their coverage of the trip was extensive, balanced and fair. (A tip to upcoming press secretaries: Don't try this with today's media—the fallout will last more than one newscycle, and you'll never live it down.)

At the end of the trip the media touring with us presented me a prized possession: a tee-shirt with the words, "We Can Play Hardball, too!" emblazed on it. We all had a good laugh as I put it on—even the *Anchorage Times* reporter.

For all of us, it was the trip of a lifetime, with the involved Interior agencies laying out the red carpet for the Secretary and his media guests. I had circulated "talking points" in advance to most of those who would be in direct contact with the press, but encouraged them all to share their thoughts candidly and openly. They all understood the "educational" goals of the trip.

As governor, Andrus had never had a security detail. When first elected, the Idaho State Police had a rotating three-person security detail for governors, but he promptly sent them back to be reassigned to highway work and traffic safety. Likewise, when he became Interior secretary he declined a security detail from either the Park Service Police or the Secret Service.

Alaska Governor Jay Hammond, however, insisted that the Secretary have at least one state trooper along because of what the Alaska State Police deemed to be serious threats to the Secretary's well-being. Reluctantly, he agreed to accede to the host governor's request.

Fortunately, Joe Hildreth, the Alaska state trooper assigned to the Secretary, handled the situation well, had a sense of Andrus' need for some privacy and a good sense of humor. They ended up being very simpatico personalities which helped to make the trip more pleasant.

The group spent the first night at the Sheffield House in Anchorage. After a cocktail reception everyone was on their own for dinner, but I did make sure we had someone from Alaska Fish & Game present at the reception so all who wanted to fish could purchase a five-day out of state fishing license.

I wanted to be sure we avoided a scenario where at least one news day would be ruined with having a Fish and Game "license check" at one of our "R & R" stops. With few or no valid fishing licenses on display, the headlines could have been ugly.

Few people realize the Department of the Interior has the eighth largest "air force" in the world in part because it operates the Interagency Fire Center in Boise. The Interagency Fire Center has numerous planes designed to fight forest and range fires throughout the West. Secondly, given the vastness of Alaska, Interior also maintains a large contingent of planes in Anchorage and Fairbanks.

Our group commandeered four aircraft for the tour: Andrus usually flew in a Grumman Goose (some insist it was a Widgeon), a classic plane designed to land on water on its belly. (If you watched *Fantasy Island*, a popular 70s-80s television show, the guests at the beginning of each episode arrived in a Goose.) Sometimes he also flew in an Aero Commander. The other two planes utilized were Cessna 404's.

The first tour day we flew for two hours north to what was the proposed Denali National Park, the dominant feature of which is Mt. McKinley, at 20,322 feet the tallest in North America. Already recognized as one of the nation's unique features, the area surrounding the mountain was one of the first designated national parks and carried the same name as the mountain. The Alaska lands legislation added some substantial acreage to the park, not to mention significantly increased funding and renamed the park, but not the mountain.

Upon landing, we boarded two buses and with an NPS naturalist journeyed deep into the park for a wonderful day of sight-seeing. Altogether, the group was able to spot and "scope" Dall sheep, moose, caribou and several large grizzly bears.

Up early the next morning, we headed for Kotzebue, a native village on the west coast. Some went via Nome and along the way overflew the proposed Koyukuk, Nowitna and Selawik national wildlife refuges. Others flew to Cape Krusenstern; others flew to Sheshalik; and still others overflew Selawik with a stop at Kiana. All of these exotic Native named places were candidates for wildlife refuge status.

While in Nome, the Secretary walked into a market on Main Street and was offered some muk-tuck from an possibly illegally-taken bowhead whale. He politely declined, but left me worrying again about the ever-present potential for bad press just by trying to be a gracious guest.

After reassembling the entire group at the Kotzebue Airport, we took buses first to a Museum of Native Art managed by the NANA Native Corporation, one of the 13 regional Native corporations established by the 1971 Alaska Native Claims Settlement Act. This stop also included watching Native dances. Then it was on to the Nul-Luk-Vik Hotel.

After a no-host dinner some walked around the town and I joined several of the journalists – Tom Brown (*Anchorage Daily News*), Jerry Lubenow (*Newsweek*) and Joel Connelly (*Seattle Post-Intelligencer*). As we strolled around we all sensed the genuine hostility towards us from virtually every native we walked by. Never before or since have I had or felt that kind of genuine hate.

One could not help feeling that the Native population in Kotzebue blamed white people for the rapid degree of change in their traditional way of life, and that the challenges of their difficult transition was a direct result of white modernization. The best example of this was the numerous number of snow-mobiles parked in front of most homes which had replaced dog-sleds. While considerably expanding their hunting range for wilderness purists the noise of any engine in a wilderness area is a transgression of the meaning of wilderness.

The next morning, Saturday, July 8, was the start largely of an "R & R" weekend. All four planes flew to Dall Creek, roughly two hours northeast of us. Along the way we overflew the Noatak National Ecological Preserve. At Dall Creek everyone was ferried by the Goose to Selby Lake, where the Park Service had set up a nice camp for us. Following a box lunch, the group could select from several options that would help them understand and appreciate recreation in the Alaska out-of-doors.

One could fish, hike or just relax at Selby Lake. Two rubber rafts and several lightweight kayaks were available. Several could fly to nearby Walker Lake for fishing and sightseeing. If one wished he could have taken a helicopter from Dall Creek and visit the Kobuk Sand Dunes before coming back to Selby Lake. I went fly fishing at Walker Lake and caught the first Arctic Grayling I'd ever lured to a fly.

Secretary Andrus canoed off to the north part of Selby Lake with a relatively new park service employee, Charles Gilbert, to fly fish for northern pike. This Chuck Gilbert was the one and the same person who so vexed Wallace McGregor later in his career as the Regional NPS land manager for acquiring in-holdings in Alaska.

The next day, Sunday, July 9, was totally devoted to outdoor activities or just relaxing at camp. Secretary Andrus did receive a belated invitation to visit a nearby mining exploration camp being run by the Anaconda Company, but he politely declined when told the press could not accompany him.

The two days and nights spent at and around Selby Lake were the highlight of a trip full of highlights. Being able to experience the beauty, serenity and solitude of the magnificent proposed Gates of the Arctic probably "sealed the deal", convincing the media accompanying us that Andrus and the Interior Department were on the correct path.

The "nights" were gorgeous even with the sun still staying slightly above the horizon. After dinner the first night, the Secretary and I took a stroll with some reporters and then sat up talking late into the night. I made only one major mistake.

In order to keep the beer ice cold we'd tied several of the cases onto a rope which we lowered into the lake from the inflatable raft it was upon. When we needed more "brewski," we would kayak out to the raft, bring another case up and cut the case loose from the main rope.

Of course, I did the one thing one is supposed to be smart enough not to do – I cut the main rope and three cases of beer settled to the bottom of Selby Lake, where I am sure they still are, ice cold and still very drinkable. Someday, when some diver comes in on a float plane to explore what she or he thinks is a pretty featureless lake, they will be rewarded with an extraordinary find.

On Monday morning we all ferried back out to Dall Creek for the leg of the trip that would take us to Prudhoe Bay for a tour of the Arco drilling facility and the start of the trans-Alaska pipeline. All the media and all the support personnel spent the day at the Arco facility. Despite fog and rain, the Secretary decided he and I would try to fly to and land at Barter Island adjacent to the eastern most Eskimo village, Kaktovik, on the North Slope. This small village, 70 miles from the border with Canada, is on the coast of the proposed Arctic National Wildlife Refuge.

Andrus was there to listen to a plea from the village elders that their subsistence way of life would be protected and that the wildlife refuge and the proposed Gates of the Arctic National Park would remain off limits to any activity including exploratory oil drilling.

The best way to achieve the highest level of protection both for the resource and the Eskimo culture was to overlay the refuge and the park with a wilderness designation. While the proposed new national park and new refuge system were closed to "outsiders" sport hunting, they still should remain open to Eskimo and Native subsistence hunting, the Eskimo elders and others in the village told Andrus.

At a minimum they wanted the coastal plain designated wilderness. The maintenance of their subsistence culture was at stake, they said, but already one could see the culture was in the midst of change with snowmobiles obviously having taken the place of long teams of huskies. Also, parked on the Barter Island airstrip were several planes presumably owned by village members.

It was a virtual certainty that both planes and snowmobiles would be used in subsistence hunting, thus ensuring the probability was high that any others traversing the area were sure to hear the sound of an engine, something that the Forest Service and the Park Service strive to avoid in the Lower 48 wilderness areas.

The village men had recently captured and legally killed a bowhead whale. The carcass of the whale was lying on the beach as we walked towards the small number of houses. Both of us were offered and tried to eat a bit of muk-tuck, a piece of raw meat cut off of the carcass, while we were standing there. Eskimos consider it a delicacy. We both found it hard to chew and swallow, but we did.

The village was nothing to write home about. A small collection of ramshackle shacks was all there was to be seen. Few of them looked sturdy enough to withstand the constant winds, but somehow they did. The brief meeting took place in the domicile of presumably the chief of the village. What I most remember was how hot the room was. It almost made one feel like he was standing in a sauna.

The villagers were warm, friendly and honored by the drop in visit from the Interior secretary. Their friendliness contrasted sharply with the palpable hostility we all felt during our earlier visit to and overnight stay at Kotzebue on the west coast of Alaska abutting the Bering Sea.

On the flight from Kaktovik to Fairbanks our pilot spotted the famed Porcupine Caribou herd, in whose name, so to speak, conservationists were arguing for preservation of the pristine environment of the Arctic National Wildlife Refuge, so that they not be impacted or impeded in their annual migration between Canada and the United States by any man-made obstacles nor should their calving grounds be disturbed.

There must have been well over a hundred thousand caribou milling about and moving on their migratory path below us. It was truly a magnificent sight, one which helped to convince the Interior secretary that most of the Arctic Wildlife range be held inviolate, one last place along the Alaska coast not to have to face the prospect even of exploratory drilling unless Congress truly deemed a national emergency dictated drilling for more oil.

It's funny, though, how the lure of money and oil can change the perspective of even those who appeared adamantly committed to preserving their old way of life. One of the reasons the issue of exploratory drilling on the coastal plain has remained a source of controversy is the good folks of Kaktovik changed their position.

One of the many compromises in the final ANILCA legislation allowed for native corporations to engage in land swaps. To the amazement of virtually all the interest groups, in 1983 the villagers of Kaktovik and their Arctic Slope regional corporation gained 92,000 acres of coastal plain land with the underlying mineral rights. Then – surprise, surprise – they reversed their position from support for designating the coastal plan and the Arctic Wildlife Refuge as Wilderness to allowing oil exploration.

In 1988 Congress closed off this loophole in an amendment to ANILCA but this first land swap orchestrated by the Reagan Administration and Interior Secretary James Watt stood. It remains a chink in the armor of all those opposed to any exploratory drilling in the last best place along the nation's extensive coastline that is mostly closed to exploratory oil and gas drilling.

The issue of whether to drill has remained controversial, unresolved and the subject of much debate ever since.

Following a day spent in meetings in Fairbanks, including one with then state senator Steve Cowper (who would go on to be elected Alaska's governor), we flew back to Anchorage with plans the following day to fly to Valdez.

Bad weather on that last day forced us to abandon plans to fly to Seward and Valdez and instead travel by bus. Early on the drive, Andrus asked the bus driver to stop for a few minutes while he darted into a liquor store.

He emerged a few minutes later carrying three cases of beer obviously intended for the media. The *Anchorage Times* reporter started to raise his camera to take a snapshot of what he knew would be an embarrassing picture of the Interior Secretary, but suddenly there were several hands in front of the lens. He got the message, lowered the camera and along with the other media enjoyed a couple of beers on our way south.

On that last day of the trip, as we chugged around a bay just out of Seward, in gorgeous sunlight with incredibly blue skies as well as a gentle breeze blowing, Andrus thanked them all for coming along and we prepared to head back to the Anchorage Airport. As a gesture of his appreciation he handed out personally inscribed copies of the then recently published *Coming Into the Country* by

John McPhee, urged them to read it and then go write about what they saw.

Write they did, with dozens of great stories showing up all across the country. My public affairs staff assembled a booklet with copies of some of the coverage which I sent to all the media with a cover note from the Secretary.

Enraged by all the positive coverage, Senator Stevens in late August hauled Secretary Andrus before the Interior Appropriations subcommittee to defend my puny (by D.C. standards) $1 million a year Public Affairs budget, the smallest Secretarial/Cabinet level budget among the cabinet agencies. West Virginia Senator Robert Byrd allowed Stevens to be the de facto chair of the subcommittee. Andrus was to defend the public affairs budget and I had to deny the charge that I had been lobbying with tax-payer funds.

Both Andrus and I contended we were educating the public, not lobbying or urging anyone else to do so.

A few years later I was bemused to learn that Stevens, when he worked at Interior as an advisor to then Secretary Fred Seaton, had himself been accused of lobbying with public funds and using federal resources available to his office to lobby for Alaska statehood. If the Secretary and I were guilty as charged, Stevens at a minimum was equally guilty.

Andrus, however, had the last word as Stevens at the hearing's end held up a copy of John McPhee's book on Alaska, and asked if Andrus had read it. Stevens clearly was thinking Andrus would answer "No," and then the Senator would administer what's known as an ad hominem lecture on the pioneer spirit of Alaskans.

*Andrus signs a copy of
Coming into the Country by
John McPhee. Photo by
National Park Service.*

Andrus replied not only had he read the book, but at that very moment the author was waiting in his office back at the Interior Department to have lunch. Andrus said he would appreciate it if Senator Stevens would adjourn the hearing so he could take care of the lunch.

It was pure serendipity, but several weeks before that I had called McPhee to invite him to come to lunch with the Secretary in his spacious office in the Interior building. It would be nothing fancy, just sandwiches in the office and a chat with the Secretary and his top staff. McPhee jumped at the opportunity. By pure accident the date turned out to be the same day of the hearing before Stevens.

The senator had little choice but to gavel the hearing to a close. As we walked out of the hearing room, Andrus was chuckling. He turned to me and said, "Chris, sometimes it pays to be lucky rather than good." I allowed myself a moment of a self-indulgent smile of satisfaction.

Other than the hearing on my budget and questions of whether I had expended federal dollars to lobby for the d-2 bill by conducting the media tour, little transpired publicly during the months of August and September after our return.

On October 4, 1978, the Senate Energy and Natural Resources Committee reported out its bill. It was completely unacceptable to the Administration, the House leadership and the Alaska Coalition. Regardless, Alaska Senator Mike Gravel still threatened to filibuster against it.

On October 12, 1978, Gravel changed course and announced he would not stand in the way of an agreement, if Senate and House conferees could hammer one out.

Behind closed doors with all the key parties present an agreement was reached on October 13. The very next day (October 14), Gravel, after reviewing the agreement, to which he had been a sporadic participant, asked for some "perfecting amendments" he knew would be unacceptable to the others inasmuch as they essentially gutted the proposed bill.

On October 15 Senator Gravel double crossed everybody by holding a press conference and essentially blowing up the agreement. Senate custom would have required unanimous consent to bring a bill to the floor that late in the session not to mention prohibiting any perfecting amendments. Senatorial courtesy permitted Gravel to put a "hold" on a bill impacting his constituents. Majority Leader Senator Robert Byrd of West Virginia was a great stickler for maintaining the traditions and customs of the Senate. Gravel and everyone knew that Byrd would not over-ride Gravel. So Gravel "took a walk".

At this point, Andrus told the conferees, "Wait a minute. Don't leave. This is going to force the President to take action to protect the d-2 lands because without legislation the earlier withdrawals will lapse at the end of this year.

"All hell will break loose in Alaska," Andrus added, and then argued for an extension of the year-end December 18, 1978 deadline. "An extension will at the least, give Congress the time to finish the bill."

He told the conferees neither he nor the President really wanted to invoke Executive Authority (meaning the Antiquities Act) to make those withdrawals, but they would if they had to do so. All the principals then agreed to a one year extension when the matter came to the floor, as scheduled, at 5:30 a.m. on October 16.

Once again, Gravel chose to grandstand, in effect telling the people of Alaska that every other party was wrong and he alone was correct. Whose interest Gravel was representing was impossible to discern. Gravel struck Andrus as one of those rogue salmon that always tries to swim upstream against the strongest part of the current just for the sake of doing so. Senator Gravel shot down the proposed extension by announcing his intention to filibuster. Congress adjourned later that day. The die was cast.

On October 17, Andrus then sent the draft supplemental EIS to the printer and ordered it released for a 30-day comment period. Through the Secretary's Office of Public Affairs I deliberately buried the lead, as my old editor, Lyle Olson, at the *Idaho State Journal* would say. I stuck the announcement on the filing of the document and the beginning of the 30-day comment period amongst a variety of various minor news-making items.

Two days elapsed before Stevens and his staff and the rest of the D.C. media tumbled to what had transpired. Stevens reportedly blew a gasket, but it was my way of once again saying to an opponent, "we can play hardball, too!"

The state of Alaska, anticipating the coming executive actions, on October 30, filed suit in Federal District Court to try to block the anticipated administrative actions by President Carter and Interior Secretary Andrus.

Then, on November 14, the state of Alaska filed land selections within the boundaries of what it knew would be some of the new national parks and wildlife refuges in the Administration's proposed bill as well as within the anticipated national monuments.

Andrus was surprised and angry for the state's action violated a promise Governor Hammond had given him that Alaska would not do that. Andrus had read Hammond as a man of his word and had accepted Hammond's personal assurances. He immediately placed a call to Hammond.

Upon reaching the governor, Hammond told Andrus that Alaska's attorney general, Avrum Gross, unaware of his governor's pledge, had unilaterally sanctioned the state action. He never even considered it possible that his governor would not *ex post facto* approve. Hammond apologized and Andrus accepted the apology recognizing that there was no way Hammond could now reverse the state's action.

On November 16, Andrus used his authority under Section 204 of the 1976 BLM Organic Act and withdrew for three years from the public domain in Alaska 110 million acres. This froze most activities on almost one third of Alaska's land and was met with howls of protest by almost all parties except conservation groups.

Later that month, on November 24 the U.S. District Court in Alaska denied the state's request for a temporary restraining order and said Andrus had acted legally. This decision freed him to recommend to President Carter that he invoke the Antiquities Act, which had always been in Andrus' mind the linchpin of the overall strategy.

Having anticipated that Gravel would throw a monkey wrench and somehow appear to have stopped if not stalled fulfillment of the d-2 promise, Andrus knew that presidential use of the Antiquities Act, which carries more restrictive regulations than most other preservation options, would prove so onerous to Alaska's delegation they would come back to the table and bargain for legislation that would undo the monument declarations. His view was validated quickly.

President Carter and his Interior secretary had correctly scoped out the moves Senator Gravel would attempt. They had arrived at a strategy, while sitting beside the gently flowing Middle Fork in Idaho, that seized the initiative from those opposed to a d-2 solution and forced them to react to their actions, not vice versus. Having a pro-active game plan ready to go must have surprised Senator Gravel despite much speculation in the media regarding utilization of the Antiquities Act by President Carter. The fact that a plan to counter Gravel's moves had been discussed by Carter and Andrus while they floated and fly fished along the Middle Fork of the Salmon in August of 1978 speaks volumes about the political acumen of both.

President Carter on December 1 designated 56 million acres as new national monuments, the largest withdrawal under the Antiquities Act in history. He also directed Andrus to take the necessary legal steps to designate the balance of the remaining lands under section 17-d-2 – some 24 million additional acres – as National Wildlife Refuges.

The burden now shifted to the opponents of fulfilling the d-2 promise and to Alaska's delegation to come up with legislation that would comply with 17-d-2. Legislation of some kind would have to be passed that would bring new additions to the four land preservation systems and remove the more restrictive language of national monument status.

Senator Stevens recognized the need for a new strategy, and so made plans to fly to Anchorage for an unscheduled meeting and fundraiser with the board of the Citizens for the Management of Alaska Lands, the umbrella opposition group. Before flying to Anchorage on December 4 he stopped in Juneau for the swearing-in ceremony for Governor Jay Hammond's second term.

Senator Stevens and his wife, Ann, along with CMAL Executive Director Tony Motley and four others then boarded a chartered Lear Jet for the trip to Anchorage.

Tragedy, however, struck. As Senator Stevens' Lear Jet was approaching its landing runway a hellacious cross wind swept through the Anchorage Airport literally flipping the jet. Ann Stevens died instantly from a broken neck and four others died with her. Somehow Senator Stevens and CMAL's Tony Motley survived. Stevens, despite his injuries, immediately left the Anchorage hospital where he had been taken, returned to the airport and caught a Frontier flight to Denver in order to personally inform Ann's father of his daughter's death before he heard about it from the local media.

I believe Stevens held Gravel personally responsible for the tragedy, and exacted some revenge. There has been some dispute over this assertion, but the evidence is strong. Two months after Ann's death, Stevens appeared before the House Interior committee shortly after the start of the 1979 session of Congress.

Newspaper accounts of the senator's testimony agree and quote him as saying the flight to Anchorage would not have been necessary if Senator Gravel had kept his word and supported the compromise.

Stevens quietly but firmly told the members of the House Interior committee, "I'm sure you realize the solution to the issue (passing the Alaska lands legislation) means more to me than it did before. I don't want to get personal about it, but I think, if that bill had passed, I might have a wife sitting at home when I get home tonight, too."

Of course Stevens did mean to get personal. Any mention of Gravel's name in his presence would bring a scowl to his face instantly. He later said his statement had been misinterpreted, but he had a funny way of saying that.

"People said I accused him of killing Ann. I was just stating a fact. We would not have gone on that plane if it were not for the fact we had to raise money. But I don't think he killed her," the Senator said.

Complicating the matter was the fact that an unknown Stevens' aide, most likely his then chief of staff, Steve Silver, excised the "intemperate" remarks from the House hearing record. Top staff is allowed to do that in order to help preserve the proper decorum whether on the House or the Senate floor or in a committee hearing.

During the spring of 1979, intensive behind the scenes work by the administration and the Alaska Coalition led to passage of a new and better House version of the Alaska lands bill. The newer, better model emerged from the House in May and passed with a solid margin of 360 votes in favor and only 65 against.

It was onto the Senate where there was finally a true champion. This senator, despite his youth and low seniority, was a man not intimidated by Senator Stevens' constant scowl. It was Massachusetts Senator Paul Tsongas.

In the early summer of 1979, Andrus and I made an additional visit to Alaska, ostensibly to do some fishing for salmon at Lake Iliamna. The trip, however, had its own profound impact on the ultimate passage of the d-2-legislation.

Early in the morning of the second day we were at the Lake Iliamna Lodge, a single engine supercharged Cessna 170 float plane landed on the still waters of the lake. It taxied over to the resort's dock where a solitary figure was waiting to be picked up. The pilot was alone. After killing the engine, he jumped out of the plane to shake hands with his passenger.

The passenger, no stranger to single engine planes, having once held a private pilot's license, was nonetheless a bit excited about the fishing trip he was being taken on by the bush pilot and guide.

The guide's name? Jay Hammond, the sitting governor of Alaska. The passenger? Cecil Andrus, the sitting secretary of the interior.

To this day few people are aware that Andrus had accepted a private invite from Hammond to spend a day fishing with him.

In 1993 Andrus told an interviewer the story, with details that made it sound like it had just happened:

"Hammond had always said, 'Sometime when you're up here, you let me know and I'll show you some of my favorite fishing places.' So, much to the consternation of all of Alaska's police officers, security police and the rest, the two of us climbed into that little Cessna of his with our fishing gear and we took off to go fishing.

"As we flew on to the first spot, Jay asked when had I first visited Alaska. Much to his surprise I told him it had been a mere four years ago that I had first come to Alaska as part of a group intent on fishing for salmon outside of King Salmon. I told him that my trip had been cut short, that while flying to fish a new place I received word that my middle daughter, Tracy, had been hospitalized with a diagnosis of Hodgkin's disease. I instructed the pilot immediately to proceed to the Anchorage airport.

"I told Governor Hammond that I had to borrow a pair of shoes because I still had my fishing waders on; and, I had to borrow some cash because while I had credit card I had no identification. Fortunately I was able without a stitch of id soever, I was able to talk my way onto a Western Airline flight to Seattle. There I was met by an Idaho Air National Guard pilot who flew me quickly to Boise and to Tracy's bedside.

"Jay and I flew around to various streams and rivers, and he'd [Hammond] land in a river – he knew them all. He'd taxi up, we'd jump out of the plane, slog around, fish for a while, and catch horrendous big old rainbow. Then he said, 'Look, you haven't had any fun until you've caught an arctic grayling on a fly in fast water.' He took me up to a place where he said there was good grayling fishing. Well, grayling is not nearly as large a fish as a big rainbow, but they have an extremely high dorsal fin. If you hook one in swift water, they'll whip that dorsal fin up, and then the fast water running against it makes you think you've got a 20-pound fish on. The fish was probably 16 to 18 inches long but it felt like you had a log on. So we had a lot of fun doing that.

"Later, we were flying along, and I, having been a little bit of a pilot myself in years gone by, looked over at the fuel gage and said, Hey, Jay, I've got news for you. Unless you've got another gas tank on here I don't know anything about, we don't have a whole hell'uv a lot of gasoline left. 'Don't fear,' he says, 'I've got some in a cache.'

"I said, What? He said, 'I keep various caches of gas cans around here in the woods in case I run a little short.' So all of a sudden he says, 'We're not very far from where I've got two five-gallon cans hidden behind a log.' I said, What if somebody has found them? 'Well,' he said, 'Then we'd have a little problem, wouldn't we?' So we land on this river, and we taxi up. It's right near where some Natives had been salmon fishing, and they were drying or curing – smoking – the salmon. So we walked up there to talk with them a little bit. He said, 'Well, nice seeing you,' and we walked a couple hundred yards down the shore and kind of ducked back in, and sure enough, there as a big old windfall tree. He leaned across it and said, 'Yup, they're still here.' And he reached in and pulled out two old GI cans that were hidden behind this log in the wet and the brush and everything.

"So I stood there thinking, They're contaminated; they have water in them; you can't tell what's happened to them. But he said, 'Don't fear.' He had a funnel in the back of the 170, and he climbed up there and took – another little trick I've learned – he took a chamois cloth like the kind you would use to dry your car, and he put it over the funnel and poured the gasoline from the old GI can through the chamois into the funnel and into the wings of the airplane. He said, 'If there's any water in there the chamois will soak it up.' Just so nonchalant. We got back in, and I say, You're not going to put those two empty cans here, are you? He said, 'Yeah, I've got to take them back and refill them and have somebody drop them off for me later.'

"So we loaded those in the back end with all our fishing gear and everything. He cranked up that Cessna, and we took off and went on about our way and ended up back at his place on Lake Clark. It was really a fun day."

After time spent fishing at several different spots, they also put down where it was sunny without wind and they spread out the map of Alaska. They then discussed the boundaries of various parts of the four systems that would make up the bulk of the Alaska lands legislation.

Hammond would point out places where the state, because of its unfinished statehood land selections, would like boundary lines put back. They also discussed access corridors for mineral sites either thought would be proved up and developed.

Andrus does not recall McGregor's Orange Hill project being raised by either of them.

Despite Andrus and Hammond's effort to reach agreements on boundaries and acreages, there was little progress for almost a year as Stevens engaged in a masterful display of how many ways a senator can stall a bill if he really wants to do so.

In the meantime, in Alaska and across the nation a conservative-led backlash against a too obtrusive federal government was building the head of steam that would fuel California Governor

Ronald Reagan's victory over President Carter in November. Nowhere was the federal government seen as too demanding, too driven by a desire to exercise social control through too many regulations, too arbitrary and capricious, than in Alaska.

Across the West aggrieved ranchers and farmers fell under the sway of hard right conservatives who wanted to privatize the federal lands, people like Reagan's first Interior secretary, attorney James Watt. They called it the "Sagebrush Rebellion" and it too helped Reagan win. It also produced bumper stickers in Alaska as well as Idaho that said: "Cece mining, cece grazing, cece logging – Cece Andrus."

Finally, on August 19, 1980, negotiations between Senators Tsongas and Jackson with the tacit agreement of Senator Stevens, who had engineered an incredible number of little and large compromises, produced a Senate bill which easily passed the Senate.

On August 26, Alaskans stunned the nation by ousting Mike Gravel in the Democratic primary.

Making things especially sweet for Senator Stevens was his quiet engineering of a massive Republican cross-over vote in Alaska's Senate primary that saw State Representative Clark Gruening, the grandson of the man Gravel defeated 12 years earlier in the 1968 Democratic primary, Senator Ernest Gruening, turn the tables and defeat Gravel.

Orchestrating any sizable Republican Party vote in the open primary of another party is a tough, challenging task. Rarely does it have the kind of impact that Stevens brought off. To my knowledge, Stevens never said a word about it. He just let the results speak for themselves.

Because Stevens never claimed he'd orchestrated a cross-over, the issue was underreported. The numbers, however, speak loudly. In the 1980 primary State Representative Clark Gruening garnered 39,719 votes to Gravel's 31,504 votes. A third Democratic contender received 1,145 votes. The total ballots cast in the Democratic primary were 72,368. There were six Republicans and Anchorage banker Frank Murkowski easily won the GOP nomination with just 16,292 votes. The total votes cast in the GOP primary were just 27,630. The turnout for the primary was 42% with approximately 102,000 votes cast.

Now let's look at senate primary races before and after 1980.

In 1978 Stevens had no primary opposition and received 83,528 votes in the Republican primary. Two Democrats were running for the right to be clobbered by Stevens in November and they received just 19,251 votes in the Democratic primary. The turnout was actually higher in 1978 than in 1980 with a 48% turnout and about 108,000 ballots cast.

Yet the GOP and Democratic primaries were mirror opposites of each other. In politics there are no coincidences.

Need further proof? In the 1984 Senate primary there were 26,268 votes cast in the Democratic primary with John Havelock winning with 19,000 votes. Stevens was again unopposed and received 65,522 votes. Thus, one sees what an anomaly the 1980 primary was and there is only one rational explanation. "Uncle Ted" got even.

Republicans then returned home politically in November and easily elected Anchorage banker Frank Murkowski (the father of current Senator Lisa Murkowski) over young Gruening. Murkowski received 84,159 votes to Gruening's 72,007. Note that Gruening's general election total was less by 300 votes than all the Democratic votes cast in the primary.

During October, the Alaska Coalition and Representative Udall pushed for additional concessions from the Senate, as many felt the Senate bill was a mere shadow of the much better House bill and that the Senate had prevailed on most disagreements with the House, but the concessions were rejected by the House and Stevens. The Alaska Coalition started to splinter and a breach opened between some elements of the coalition and the administration. Some in the coalition wanted to wait and take their chance with the new Congress.

On November 4, the Alaska Coalition and conservationists everywhere received the wake up call: President Carter lost his bid for re-election.

The Alaska Coalition recognized the fact that chances for any bill in the new Congress, with a new Republican president, would be nil. They conceded as much and receded. Several technical amendments slightly delayed final passage.

At long last, on December 1, 1980, the Alaska National Interest Lands Conservation Act, Public Law 96-487, was enacted by the Senate.

On December 2, 1980, President Jimmy Carter, in a ceremony in the East Room of the White House, signed the greatest piece of conservation law in history, an unparalleled legacy for future generations. The first pen used to sign the bill was handed to the quarterback, Interior Secretary Cecil D. Andrus. That simple gesture said it all.

The bill may have had a thousand fathers and mothers, but the Final Father of the Alaska lands bill will for all time be remembered as President Jimmy Carter. Many would also say the First Presidential Father was Theodore Roosevelt.

On the day President Carter signed the Alaska lands legislation Andrus held a reception to celebrate the success and thank all the many employees throughout the department who had contributed to the effort. On the stage behind the lectern he had a blackboard placed and he had written upon it an old saying: "Success has a thousand fathers and mothers. Failure is a bastard."

He stood before dozens of folks who had been working for this success outside of the Interior department, as well as hundreds of employees "inside" who were beginning to revere this balding former lumberjack from Orofino, Idaho. They recognized they had an extraordinary boss. He, in turn, recognized he had an unusually hard-working and dedicated group of public servants. One could sense in the room the satisfaction on the part of all over this historic accomplishment.

It was a success that truly did have a thousand fathers and mothers, and many agencies played key roles besides the Interior Department and its bureaus. The U.S. Forest Service, the Coast Guard, the newly created Environmental Protection Agency, the National Oceanic and Atmospheric Agency, the environmental division of the Justice Department, the Council on Environmental Quality, to name a few, all played their parts and played them well.

Within the Interior Department, the National Park Service, the Bureau of Land Management, the Fish & Wildlife Service, the U.S. Geological Survey, and the Bureau of Indian Affairs had hundreds of good, solid public servants who were proud to play their part and who performed exceptionally well.

Too modest to claim President Carter could not have done it without him, Andrus has to know a large part of the credit belongs to him, his leadership, skills, intelligence, and ability to see over the horizon. Andrus also knows no one would have been able to achieve their success had it not been for the Alaska Coalition and the heavy lifting performed by Doug Scott, Brock Evans and Chuck Clusen.

The bill stands today as one of the greatest – perhaps the greatest – conservation accomplishment in our nation's history.

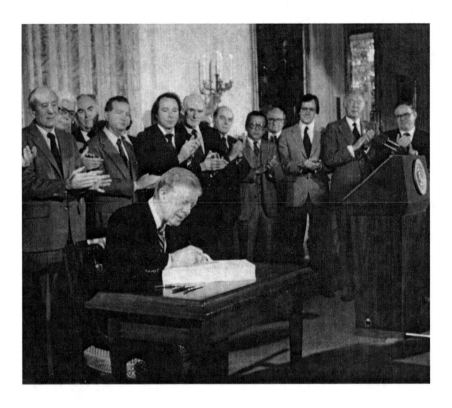

*President Jimmy Carter signs the Alaska lands bill. Photo courtesy of the Carter Library.*

# Part 2

# Consequences

# 5

# Early diggings

*Wallace McGregor (above), photo by Serena Carlson. Chuck Gilbert, in a spoof of developers, sits in an abandoned d-7 Cat (below) photo by National Park Service.*

For every action there is an opposite but equal reaction, Sir Isaac Newton posited several centuries ago, formulating one of the fundamental laws of physics.

In the real world of politics that law is transformed into what most political practitioners and observers would call "the law of unintended consequences."

A rephrasing of Newton's law in the political world would read: "For every well-intended law passed by any legislative body, inevitably there is an unfortunate, unintended consequence that causes great harm."

The Alaska National Interest Lands and Conservation Act is no exception. Passage of the law created difficult situations for any number of Alaskans who owned private property within the national parks and preserves. Some of these in-holders, fully aware of their constitutional right to be fairly compensated if there were a taking of their property by government, were willing to sell to the federal government, but full funding was rarely available.

For the vast majority of in-holdings, however, there's no intention of government acquisition.

Some agreements permit in-holders lifetime occupancy rights, followed by turnover to the federal agency. Others were resolved by outright sale. Likewise, within many of the new parks, wildlife refuges, monuments and wilderness areas one could often find valid, privately owned, proven up mining claims.

Title 11 of ANILCA, as well as the Mining in the Parks Act, mandates that the predominant federal land management agency provide authorization for overland access to these in-holdings and proven up mining claims. The federal agency by law has other criteria besides access by which it evaluates the private property before offering a price. The result is often protracted negotiations.

A major factor impacting the acquisition of these private pieces of property is of course the availability, or lack, of funds for purchasing these properties. The dollars primarily come from the government's Land and Water Conservation Fund. Most voters do not realize the source of the money is the bids paid by oil companies for the right to drill for oil and gas offshore.

Congress then allocates and appropriates the dollars to specific proposed acquisitions. Funds available for acquisitions often fluctuate depending on the nation's overall economy and of course priorities mandated by the respective chairs of the Senate and House Appropriations Committees.

Fortunately for Alaska, for many years the Republican senator with the most seniority, and the chair at times of the Senate Appropriations committee was none other than their state's senior senator, Ted Stevens.

On the House side, Alaska's at-large congressman, Don Young, likewise became the Republican member with the most seniority. At times, then, the spigot was opened fairly wide, and priority in-holdings were purchased and property owners compensated.

The process of establishing values for these in-holdings and proven up mineral properties is of necessity a difficult and lengthy one. It is the taxpayers' dollars, and agency public land managers have a fiduciary responsibility to ensure funds aren't expended for properties which are over-valued by their owners.

When it comes to acquiring in-holdings basic steps include an extensive valuation study usually based on comparable properties and full-blown appraisals of subsurface minerals. The process is undoubtedly cumbersome. Different people have had different reactions as to how well the process works.

One man who to this day feels violated and believes his constitutional right to the beneficial use of his property was taken away by the National Park Service is Wallace McGregor – the same man who flew into Alaska to evaluate the feasibility of Kennecott Copper beginning operations in that state, described in chapter one.

McGregor is a decent and honorable person, tall and lean with piercing eyes. He possesses even in his late 80s a razor sharp intellect and resonates rectitude, as well as tenacity tempered with common sense. He also manifests the zeal of a true believer in business.

He has come to believe the NPS is ignoring the U.S. Constitution.

Sitting across the table from McGregor on many occasions was a veteran National Park Service employee named Charles (Chuck) Gilbert, head of the Lands Division for the NPS's Alaska regional office. To talk with Chuck Gilbert is to find a reasonable, conscientious employee, trying to do his job as well as he can.

The trench warfare running through that table has been going on for more than 30 years.

Wallace McGregor was born in West Orange, New Jersey, on April 12, 1928, the only child of Wallace McGregor, Sr., and Naomi Witte. He described his childhood as uneventful and fairly normal. He has no memory of hardship or hunger during the Depression. He was graduated from Red Bank High School in New Jersey a year after the close of World War II, in May of 1946.

While the nation's military then was in a massive drawdown mode, the services still needed recruits to replace veterans opting out and heading home. McGregor chose the Navy over the other services because, while growing up on the East Coast, he developed a strong interest in shipping. Watching freighters move along through Chesapeake Bay, or naval vessels chugging toward the Philadelphia Naval Shipyard for repairs, always thrilled him, and left him wondering where the vessels had been or would be going. Besides having spent a great deal of time near the water, a high school buddy of his also wanted to join the Navy, so they enlisted together. McGregor later said when talking about joining the Navy, it is always easier to make a life-altering decision if one has a buddy along.

McGregor's buddy was a ham radio buff, and involved extensively with radio communications. Both applied for the ETM (Electronics Technicians Mate) program. McGregor was surprised when he was selected and his buddy was not. Thus, they went their separate ways, as is often the case in the service, and never crossed paths again.

McGregor was stationed on a submarine tender, the *U.S.S. Orion*. Submarine tenders are basically floating convenience stores, stocked with food, merchandise, and any equipment a submarine needs, they have become fairly large vessels that tag along with a flotilla of other ships, or with a battle group if the exercise is large enough.

The idea of Alaska first caught McGregor's attention in 1947, while he was stationed in the Panama Canal Zone. He came across a book in the ship's library entitled *Alaska: Land of Tomorrow*, written by E. A. Herron, which ignited his interest in Alaska. Further browsing in the ship's library led him to another gem, a textbook on geology. The more he delved into the subject, the more interested he became, perhaps because it fit so well with the attraction of Alaska. Could the humidity and heat of the Canal Zone have inspired thoughts of cold, windswept Arctic highlands with drifting snow, igloos and Eskimos as an alternative environment?

The books got him hooked, and he knew what he wanted to study at college. By the time McGregor completed his naval service, he was already enrolled at the Colorado School of Mines.

In June 1948, McGregor received his honorable discharge from the Navy. Before heading to Golden, McGregor received a letter from a Colorado School of Mines student, Bill Hogan, whom he'd never met though Hogan was from his hometown and had attended the same high school. Hogan was one of those classic gung-ho for the alma mater types that every campus seems to have. He was also a member of the Sigma Phi Epsilon fraternity, and adept at identifying and recruiting incoming freshmen for his fraternity. Hogan commended McGregor on his selection of CSM and gave him his phone number encouraging him to call when he arrived in Golden. McGregor initially decided to ignore the note.

McGregor headed west by train to Denver marveling at the vastness of the United States along the way; from Denver he boarded the Golden Goose, a trolley that ran to Golden following the meandering course of Clear Creek. It was a memorable trip for a young man with geology on his mind, since the course of the creek cut a channel through a basalt flow creating the prominent topographical features of the area – the North and South Table mountains.

When McGregor arrived in Golden, he decided after all to give Hogan a call. Hogan invited him to meet at the fraternity house and in the course of the meeting, offered McGregor a place to stay until he found more permanent lodging. McGregor accepted, and the Sigma Phi Epsilon House became his residence during the rest of the time he was at the School of Mines.

McGregor learned that an education at CSM went well beyond book learning and the classroom. In looking back, he attributed the fortunate launching of his CSM learning experience to the happenstance of Bill Hogan writing him that first letter. Another fortunate happenstance was being assigned to Ed Gaulke, another pledge, as a roommate. Gaulke came to CSM on a full football scholarship and getting to know him heightened McGregor's interest in turning out for the CSM football team. In high school he had not been able to make the team. At CSM, he walked on and made the freshman team. By his junior year he was a starter on offense with a specialty in returning kickoffs and punts. McGregor also lettered in track and swimming.

In his senior year, the opening football game was in Pocatello against Idaho State University. Playing in the old Spud Bowl (the more recent MiniDome would not be constructed until the late 60's), McGregor took the opening kickoff and started up field. His football career ended in a split second as he was hammered by a career-ending tackle that severely injured his left thigh. He was on crutches for over a month and never made it back to the playing field. Without any contribution from McGregor, CSM went on to win the 1951 Rocky Mountain Conference championship.

A picture taken of McGregor before the injury shows a tall, lean and  no-nonsense young man with dark hair, steel blue eyes clearly set on making a mark in the world, and a scowl that says, don't mess with me.

In 1999, the 1951 team was inducted into CSM's Athletic Hall of Fame with many of the team members coming back to campus for the induction ceremony. Indicative of the esteem McGregor earned while playing football was an invitation to him from the members of that championship team to attend and participate. McGregor proudly accepted.

While at CSM, McGregor also joined Theta Tau, a professional engineer's fraternity, served as president for one year of the Delta Chapter of Sigma Phi Epsilon, and served as student body treasurer his junior year.

In his senior year McGregor was awarded the W.A. Tarr Citation by the Sigma Gamma Epsilon professional fraternity. The award is given annually to the single student, "in recognition of Scholarship and Professionalism in the Earth Sciences." Considering he was a member of the competing fraternity of engineers the award came as a complete surprise to him.

Another important aspect of the CSM learning experience was the summer field courses. These were, and still are, integral elements of the education at CSM. These field courses included such classes as field surveying, mine surveying and geologic field courses. The courses covered all three summers after McGregor's arrival at CSM.

The summer between his junior and senior year he was able to do a "short course" and a job that gave him his first taste of Alaska.

In the spring of 1951, McGregor saw an opportunity for summer employment with the Alaska Road Commission. He brought the opportunity to the attention of a schoolmate, Ned Tarbox. Together, they applied for the summer work and were both hired on for the summer. They were assigned to a construction site near Copper Center, Alaska.

McGregor cherishes the memory of his first "coming into the country." Like most, he was overwhelmed by its beauty and in awe of its vastness, a "love at first sight." He knew almost from the first instant that he wanted to spend as much of his life as possible exploring and getting to know this incredible part of the Earth.

The work was hard manual labor, and McGregor took to it with his usual enthusiasm. It also reinforced for both him and Tarbox, though, their desire to obtain their college degrees.

The most memorable event of the summer involved Tarbox and McGregor neglecting one of the basic rules for survival in or near a wilderness.

The Road Commission had a camp for employees that they stayed in for a few days, but a little more independence appealed to them, so they set up a sleeping tent in a wooded area apart from the Road Commission camp. All went well for a couple of weeks until one night McGregor was awakened by a heavy nudge to his cot and the rattle of a coffee can.

When he rolled over to see the source of the noise, he was face to face with the rump of a bear standing on top of Tarbox's sleeping bag while it batted around a can of salmon scraps left over from their evening meal. Fortunately, Tarbox was on the night shift. McGregor wisely elected to do nothing but watch. Once the bear was satisfied that it had gotten all the salmon it could, it exited the tent the way it came in, which, as he was to learn from later experiences, was not generally the exit procedure. It was a lesson learned. Thereafter, they cached their food and garbage well away from their tent.

When McGregor graduated from the Colorado School of Mines in May of 1952, employment opportunities were exceptionally good. From his perspective, it was more a matter of choosing the employer than being selected for employment. He chose a company with a history of mining in Alaska – Kennecott Copper Company.

At the time, Kennecott was in the process of beefing up its exploration activities and had organized an exploration subsidiary, Bear Creek Mining Co. In accepting employment with Bear Creek, McGregor made clear his interest in Alaskan exploration. As a result, he was assigned to the Northwest District office in Spokane.

The choice proved to be all McGregor could ask for when, at the outset of the 1953 field season, he was assigned to investigate a property called Orange Hill, located in the Wrangell Mountain Range of Alaska. The site consisted of 18 patented mining claims and one patented mill site, and encompassed 363 acres. The site was at the terminus of the Nabesna Glacier, about 12 miles from the village of Nabesna.

Accompanied by a senior geologist, a college student summer employee, and a resident of McCarthy, Alaska, hired to serve as cook and camp manager, McGregor and crew flew by bush plane to Orange Hill, where they landed on a gravel bar along the Nabesna River.

They quickly hauled their camp gear up to a location central to the mineralization behind Orange Hill and set up camp. McGregor couldn't know this site would become a consuming, indeed, a defining passion for much of the rest of his life.

# 6

# Orange Hill

ORANGE HILL
Elevation 2875 estimated
N61 12.00/W142 51.00 estimated
Photo Date Summer 1969

1600 X 30

Nabesna
River

Nabesna
Glacier

Airstrip condition unknown.
Landing area may be overgrown
and/or abandoned.

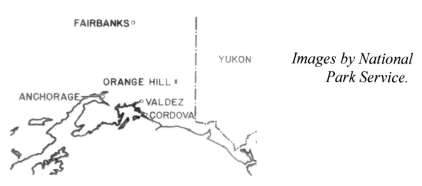

FAIRBANKS○

YUKON

ORANGE HILL ▪

ANCHORAGE

VALDEZ
CORDOVA

*Images by National
Park Service.*

After his initial analysis at Orange Hill in 1953, Wallace McGregor was convinced that he had rediscovered "the mother lode," a site full of minerals worth several billion dollars. In 1968 he was able to acquire the site for a mere $25,000. His Brown & Root corporate partners bought in several years later, it appears, for around $500,000 for their one third share. Work on the site proceeded, on and off for years.

Chuck Gilbert came to Alaska in 1976 and hired on with the National Park Service that same year. He was involved in some of the initial planning for the new d-2 lands but did not switch to the Land Management/Purchase department until the mid-1980s; it was then he became acquainted with McGregor.

Gilbert would describe their differences from the mid-80s to today as a wide gap in valuing the site and whether it was truly economic to develop it.

McGregor defined the differences as a Park Service assault on private property rights.

In 2005, former President Ronald Reagan's attorney general, Edwin Meese III, commented in a *Wall Street Journal* article ("The Property Rights Test", August 2, 2005), "Few constitutional protections are less ambiguous than the requirement that private property must not be taken for public use 'without just compensation.'" McGregor would argue that Meese cast his words in the wrong tense, that he easily could have cited the famous statement made in 1775 by one of the stalwart Virginia patriots, Arthur Lee: "The right of property is the guardian of every other right, and to deprive the people of this is in fact to deprive them of their liberty."

What was held to be an unambiguous right in the minds of the drafters of the Fifth Amendment has today become, to McGregor and many others, tenuous. McGregor points to the fact he and his partners have yet to reach any negotiated settlement with the National Park Service on their claim of a taking some 40 years later.

McGregor has kept a historical record of the case over the years, and he believes it shows a deliberate disregard for the law by NPS. Chuck Gilbert points to the same record and argues it shows McGregor's unwillingness to accept the legal criteria the Park Service must follow in acquiring in-holdings and the appraisal process it must go through beforehand. The difference is less over fact – though there's some of that too – than over interpretation.

The Fifth Amendment says that private property shall not "be taken for public use without just compensation." The Fourteenth Amendment states "nor shall any State deprive any person of life, liberty, or property without due process of law."

An old saying holds that private property marks the boundary between the citizen and the state. In his excellent 1994 book, *Lost Rights: The Destruction of American Liberty*, James Bovard wrote, "The degree of respect the State shows for property rights will largely determine how much privacy, autonomy and independence the citizen has. Property is the exclusive right to use and dispose of an object or idea."

As far back as 1917 the U.S. Supreme Court stated: "Property is more than the mere thing which a person owns. It is elementary that it includes the right to acquire, use and dispose of it. The Constitution protects these essential attributes of property."

McGregor's case tests this idea.

Mining activity at Orange Hill began by 1902 when, according to the U.S. Geological Survey, "A large number of claims have already been staked on California Gulch in the vicinity of Orange Hill."

Bud Sergeant, one of Alaska's many early and colorful miners, placer-mined the gulch from 1911 through 1922. He sold his claims in 1923 to the Alaska Nabesna Corporation, a company organized by a successful Washington, D.C., real estate investor, James Dulin. From 1924 through 1928, the Alaska Nabesna Corporation conducted exploration by driving adits and diamond drilling, in the course of which it staked additional claims covering the Orange Hill disseminated mineralization and areas of skarn mineralization in the limestone.

In 1928, the Alaska Nabesna Mining Company patented 18 mineral claims and one five-acre mill site at Orange Hill, comprising a total of 363 acres. When the Great Depression hit in 1932, exploration was halted and thereafter, the property remained dormant until the early 1950s, when interest in Alaskan exploration was renewed.

In 1953 McGregor, as a 25-year-old Kennecott geological engineer, first heard of the Orange Hill property and, following his expedition elsewhere in Alaska with Ed Owen, was assigned by the company to make a quick visit there to assess the site.

It was a true backcountry experience.

Every day at Orange Hill there were sightings of Dall sheep grazing on the mountain side above, below, and sometimes beside them. The number of Dall Sheep is in fact the primary reason Orange Hill ended up in a "park preserve" which permits sport hunting as well as subsistence hunting. Occasionally, a moose would be spotted in the flats along the river below. Initially McGregor and his crew carried rifles for bear protection, but after a while, without any sightings of bear, they decided the precaution was unnecessary, which is when Murphy's Law stepped in.

On the day they chose not to carry their rifles, when they returned to camp the cook told them he'd seen a bear come out of the bush down the trail shortly after they had gone up the trail. They didn't encounter that bear, but did opt for the inconvenience of carrying their rifles.

At the completion of mapping, McGregor and crew took time to prospect an area of varicolored oxidized mineralization on Nikonda Creek, a drainage located to the southeast of Orange Hill. For McGregor, it was an enjoyable foray into the "high country" behind Orange Hill and an ideal way to wrap up his first experience there.

McGregor thought it would be the last that he'd see of Orange Hill, but in fact, 1953 would prove to be the first of many field seasons he would enjoy there. His involvement over the years that followed would range from geological consultant to owner, to that of joint venture owner during the course of which the intensity of exploration increased during the decade of the 1970s.

A letter was waiting for McGregor when he returned to the Spokane office from that first trip to Orange Hill. It was from one of his Colorado geology professors, Dr. K.S. Herness, who had introduced McGregor to geologic field mapping. The letter was an offer of employment with Herness' consulting firm, Minerals Exploration Research Corporation, which was focused on the highly competitive field of uranium exploration.

McGregor's first inclination was to say, "Thanks, but no thanks." Yet, he found something compelling about the offer, and while the decision was difficult, he decided to accept. Before heading to his new field office, McGregor completed reports from notes on his Alaska explorations in November, 1954, and then headed to Grand Junction, Colorado, where his new field office was located.

Previous experience in uranium exploration had opened his eyes to the joy of working for one's self that independent work brought. In addition, several bad experiences in an industry heavily infested with unscrupulous promoters drilled home the lesson that it was going to take more than geologic know-how and luck to succeed; it was going to take some business acumen. It became clear to him that he needed basic business education, and that graduate study in business administration was a necessity. McGregor decided to seek more education, applied to the Harvard Business School, was accepted, and began his graduate studies in September of 1956.

When it came to locating a summer job at the end of the first year, one of his professors, Dr. Hugh McKinstry, helped him gain employment as a mining geologist at a mine in Chibougamau, Quebec, Canada. It was a job that he truly enjoyed.

Within days of his graduation from the Harvard Business School McGregor headed back west. Returning to Alaska would take time, but he was back on the path.

During the 1960s, when McGregor's involvement in Alaskan exploration expanded, his income was derived primarily from geologic consulting during the off-season. One of his geological consulting relationships was with James Hogle, whom he came to know during the early 1960s, while living in Salt Lake City. Hogle was president of the J. A. Hogle Co., an investment brokerage firm organized by his father in 1914, and he had an abiding interest in mining. His investments were astute and resulted in his holding controlling interest in several operating mines.

One of his companies was the Consolidated Eureka Mining Company. Its mine was located close to Eureka, Nevada. In 1965, the company was conducting a drilling program funded by the Defense Minerals Exploration Administration, a federal program, referred to as DMEA. Hogle asked McGregor to supervise the project. The objective appeared to be for the nation's military to have a good understanding of where to locate the minerals that contribute key components to the defense industry. If a key strategic metal, for example, was suddenly in short supply the nation had to have at its fingertips an idea of where to find more.

For McGregor, the "supervision" involved little more than overseeing a one-rig diamond drilling project, as agreed at the outset with the DMEA. The project's purpose was to test the depth of the extension of mineralization. The time required to oversee the drilling was minimal, leaving the major portion of his time to study the area's geology. McGregor did this by geologically mapping every drift and mine working that was accessible from previous mining.

By the time the DMEA drilling program was completed without success, he had geologically mapped thousands of feet of mine workings from which he had drawn some conclusions concerning the natural structural forces that determined the locations of the caves. If his conclusions were correct, that the mineralization was associated within, McGregor postulated that all that was needed to locate ore was to locate the open caves by means of long-hole drilling.

McGregor presented his geologic findings to Hogle and proposed that he undertake a simple long-hole drilling program from existing workings to test specific locations for open caves. Hogle, a very savvy individual, but not a geologist, questioned the likelihood of success and declined to take the risk.

Though disappointed, McGregor was too confident in his conclusions to give up. He offered to take the risk himself, with a proposal to conduct the drilling at his own expense under a lease agreement providing a royalty on production to Consolidated

Eureka Mining Company in the event of success. Hogle accepted this proposal.

McGregor turned immediately to long-hole drilling, and within weeks located three caves. Plans were made to access the caves by drilling from the nearest established workings.

After setting up the drill program, he returned to Salt Lake City to await results. Shortly thereafter, the mine manager called to report having broken into a cave. This ultimately led to a profitable endeavor for McGregor.

Alaska, however, was always at the front of his mind. One fortunate benefit from operating the Eureka Mine was it provided employment during the Alaskan off-season for a key employee, Phil Grubaugh, McGregor's master mechanic. Grubaugh was responsible for the operation and maintenance of a dozer and several other vehicles in Alaska. His talents were equally valuable to McGregor at the Eureka mine, so he was pleased he could provide Grubaugh with a secure annual income that ensured his availability when needed in Alaska.

Grubaugh moved to Eureka from his home in Arizona and for several years thereafter headed to Alaska by truck each May, hauling repair parts and items needed to maintain the equipment on the exploration projects in Alaska.

Little did McGregor realize at the time that during the course of exploration at the Consolidated Eureka mine major changes were taking place in mine safety at the federal level. McGregor ran head first into, in his view, the increasingly oppressive hand of federal regulatory agencies. He was simply baffled at the "feds" inability to apply common sense to their increasingly intrusive regulations. McGregor later felt it was a harbinger and a foreshadowing of what would be coming down the pike in Alaska.

In 1968, he bought into the Orange Hill property for $25,000.

Nationally, 1968 saw the assassinations of Martin Luther King and Robert F. Kennedy, as well as the return of Richard Nixon to the political scene and a consequent acceleration of the war in Vietnam. In Alaska, the year saw a changing of the guard in the Senate with

Mike Gravel defeating Ernest Gruening in the Democratic primary and then winning the general, and Ted Stevens succeeding Bob Bartlett upon Bartlett's early December death. Only months later, Walter J. Hickel left the governorship to become Nixon's Interior Secretary, and was succeeded by Keith Miller. The year also saw the discovery of oil at Prudhoe Bay and the rise in demands by Alaska's natives for a fair settlement to their land claims.

McGregor believes that had he not felt property rights were secure during the 1960s and 1970s, he would have had no incentive to strike out to prospect in Alaska. Nor would he have been able to organize Northwest Explorations (which he did with the support of George R. Brown, co-founder of the Brown & Root Company, the predecessor company to KBR which also owns Halliburton). McGregor's analysis of the value of the minerals present in Orange Hill led him to believe it to be among the top 15 percent largest copper deposits in the world.

*George Brown*

George Brown is one of the most remarkable business figures of the 20th century. The star beneficiary of the Brown brothers' political support over many years was none other than Lyndon Baines Johnson, still president in 1968. The Browns' extensive history with LBJ and key support for him early in his career is well documented in Robert Caro's massive multi-volume Johnson biography.

McGregor said he was introduced by a mutual friend to Brown on a visit to Houston in a "happenstance," and that the two of them hit it off. Much in the world of business and politics is all about the relationships one develops and nurtures along the way. In this case, a George Brown employee named Bill Tonking introduced the two. At the time, Tonking was an engineer employed by Brown & Root and was working in Wyoming. McGregor and he had a chance meeting in the spring of 1970 when Tonking stopped by to investigate an experimental oil production project that McGregor and a fellow investor, Bob Trent, were conducting on a shallow oil field that lacked the energy to drive the oil in the ground to the drill holes.

McGregor said the process involved the application of mining technology to the production of oil from drilling horizontal holes from a shaft that intersected the oil bearing formation at a depth of about 200 feet. In the course of explaining the process to Tonking, McGregor mentioned the Orange Hill project and his plans being developed for further exploration.

A few weeks later, McGregor received a phone call from Tonking asking if he would meet with George Brown to discuss the Orange Hill project. Shortly thereafter, McGregor was in Houston meeting with Brown and Ed Williamson, the president of the Louisiana Land and Exploration Company. The meeting's outcome was the organization of Northwest Explorations Joint Venture with the participation of the Louisiana firm and the George R. Brown Partnership together with the AJV Company and Brown & Root.

McGregor felt good about Brown & Root becoming a one-third partner. When things proved difficult, Brown & Root could easily have walked away when matters became stuck in the maw of federal bureaucracy, but Brown remained a partner throughout the many years McGregor struggled with the Park Service.

In recent years, the successor entity to Brown & Root, KBR, has been the holder of the one-third share. In 2012, some company officials moved toward pulling out of the project, but the George Brown family trust supported McGregor and stayed in.

The organization was subject to the provisions of Subchapter K of Chapter 1 of Subtitle A of the U.S. Internal Revenue Code of 1954. The organizing participants were McGregor's privately held company, AJV Corporation; the Louisiana Land & Exploration

Company; Brown & Root, Inc.; and, Highland Resources, Inc., a closely-held family company of George R. Brown's.

McGregor later changed the name of his firm to Geo-Enterprise, Inc., headquartered in Spokane. The Louisiana Land & Exploration Company was a New York Stock Exchange-listed company, which was subsequently merged into Echo Bay Mines, Inc. Brown & Root, Inc. (now known as Kellogg, Brown & Root, Inc. or KBR, of which Halliburton Co. is a wholly owned subsidiary) was a private company organized by the Brown brothers, Herman and George.

In 1984, the mineral and petroleum assets of Highland Resources, Inc. were merged into the George R. Brown Partnership. In 1998, the interest of Louisiana Land & Exploration Company/Echo Bay was acquired by the remaining partners in the Joint Venture.

As mentioned earlier, in the tumultuous year that was 1968, McGregor had purchased the Orange Hill site for $25,000. When George Brown bought in for a third interest in 1970 the Joint Venture was organized with $500,000 cash for a 51% interest to Brown and others, and McGregor's contribution was the property and some other properties valued in total at $480,392 or a 49% interest. McGregor said there was a second go round on investment and his 49% interest was valued at $1,470,000.

The fact that he acquired the Orange Hill site for approximately $25,000 suggests the previous owners did not view its prospects so favorably. That was a point contributing to Chuck Gilbert's questions about the property's value.

McGregor also puts stock in an agreement he and his partners had with U.S. Borax in 1977, in which that firm entered into an Option to Purchase. Were the right to mine the Orange Hill deposit not considered a certainty in 1977, McGregor believes U. S. Borax & Chemical Co. would not have entered into that agreement with he and his partners. Later, they walked away, recognizing the new reality was they never would be able to develop an economically feasible and sustainable mine operation.

Wallace McGregor was active in both the Alaska Mining Association and was twice president of the Northwest Mining Association. Both associations were against fulfilling the 17-d-2 obligation and were implacable in their opposition. McGregor in later years speculated the hostility he felt visited upon him by the Park Service was in part due to his having been an officer in both. Gilbert says there is no truth to such speculation.

Senator Ted Stevens had promised several times to take care of the mining industry, and in a general sense he did. All the various public land withdrawals executed by the Interior Department, with the exception of the Native claims, and future withdrawals, allowed miners to continue to locate minerals, prove up and patent claims.

The final Alaska Native Claims Settlement Act contained language that seems clear and direct: "Any mining claim within those withdrawals which had been initiated before August 31, 1971 was protected." It also said that anyone who made a lawful entry onto public lands before August 31, 1971 would have his interest protected until he had time to perfect his claim. The final bill was of course a set of complex compromises, but there was another section which guaranteed access for mining projects that could demonstrate economic feasibility.

McGregor contended everything changed on November 16, 1978, when, at the behest of Secretary Andrus, President Carter used his power under the Antiquities Act and created a 56-million acre Alaskan wilderness withdrawal. What would become the Wrangell-St. Elias National Park constituted 10,950,000 acres of the 56 million.

McGregor claims this effectively closed the Wrangell Range to mining, though Gilbert points out that one could still mine under the Mining in the Parks Act.

The ultimate purpose of the withdrawal was to get the "Crown Jewel" lands into a protected state, much of the acreage under a strict wilderness designation. The massive withdrawal, moreover, served to motivate Alaskan Senator Ted Stevens and the Alaska congressional delegation to get behind a bill that would undo the Antiquities Act designation to be replaced by more appropriate designations, such as national parks or wildlife refuges.

Stevens was one of the Senate's most shrewd parliamentarians. Only Majority Leader Robert Byrd of West Virginia, to whom Stevens was close to despite their partisan differences, knew the Senate rules better. Thus, far more successfully than Representative Young on the House side, Stevens was able to use the rules and the tricks of the trade to stall any Alaska lands legislation reaching the Senate floor for two full years.

After Stevens' two-year stall, in December, 1980, the Senate enacted the Alaska National Interest Lands Conservation Act. The Act created, among the various new national parks, the Wrangell-St. Elias National Park, in which the Orange Hill property was enclosed. At 13.2 million acres, the WRST became and remains the largest park in the national park system, comparable in size to the entire country of Switzerland.

An adjoining "sister park" located in Canada makes WRST even larger. WRST has been designated as one of the world's outstanding "International Parks." Denali National Park (surrounding Mt. McKinley) and the Gates of the Arctic National Park are, along with Wrangell-St. Elias, considered to be a trio of major parks.

McGregor said from this point forward the Park Service in general and Gilbert in particular became more aggressive in disregarding his right as a private property owner.

In later responding to the charge, Gilbert countered that the lands staff respected everyone's property rights.

Stevens took up the cause, but primarily focused on those privately owned lands within the new Denali National Park. McGregor thought Stevens seemed to forget the same issue existed in the other proposed parks, particularly WRST. Unlike the other parks, Denali in-holders were far more numerous and many were Alaska residents. It became a classic case of the squeaky wheel getting the grease.

When the Eureka mine closed, McGregor had decided to move to Spokane in the spring of 1971. It was an easy decision because he had a fondness for Spokane, having lived there during the first days out of college in 1952-54 while working for Bear Creek

Mining Co. Also importantly, Spokane was becoming a congregating point for exploration geologists. With the Alaskan exploration going well, Spokane was a logical choice as home base for Alaskan exploration.

McGregor reported to his partners at their 1973 annual meeting that following a rough start, exploration began to go well at Orange Hill during the 1973 field season. In particular, he was encouraged by events that had occurred in Washington, D.C., almost two years earlier with the passage of the Alaska Native Claims Settlement Act.

While he was aware the driver for the settlement act was the desire of the oil industry to begin to tap into the great pool of oil that had been discovered in the Prudhoe Bay area of Alaska's North Slope, and the need to convey that oil via a pipeline to an ice free port like Valdez on the southern coast of Alaska, neither he nor his attorneys focused on the standard boiler plate language that everything in the act was subject to valid existing rights. In addition, they did not understand that the lands at Orange Hill might be withdrawn under Section 17(d)2 of ANCSA, for the possible establishment of a national park.

Initially carrying the load for Senator Stevens on making sure in-holders rights were respected and protected in any future legislation establishing new parks or refuges was his legislative director, John Katz, who had migrated to Stevens' staff following the defeat of his previous boss, Alaska Congressman Howard Pollock, in the 1970 Republican gubernatorial primary (won by Walter Hickel).

During the 1970s, and leading up to the passage of ANILCA, Katz worked closely with the Alaska Miners Association and Washington Senator Henry Jackson's staff to get language in the bill affirming even more strongly one's patented mining claims. Title 11 of ANILCA is clear on the need for the National Park Service to authorize access to patented, proven up and economically viable mining projects.

McGregor said when he became aware of this he was even more pleased that his efforts – the blood, sweat and tears – would not go unrewarded. McGregor confirmed also, that he was well aware there was serious interest within the Department of the Interior to come up with some plan, either a wilderness or a national park, for the Wrangell-St. Elias Mountains. Actions like that of Senator Stevens and the Alaska Mining Association served to reassure him, however.

When McGregor and those he had contracted with to assist during the 1973 field season first arrived at their work camp in May, they discovered a bear, or several bears, had thoroughly ransacked the camp. A portion of the wall of the core shed had been torn off and havoc wrought on the washhouse.

The core shed (where core samples from drilling holes were stored) damage was minor with just a sheet of plywood having been removed and only a bear's paw could squeeze through the entrance. The consequence was just a couple of core boxes had been pulled out, and there was no real loss because each core sample was numbered. The boxes were easily reorganized and reassembled.

As to the washhouse, the problem was not so much a matter of repairing damage as it was one of restoring order. To gain entrance, the bear(s) had chosen to tear off the door, which was far more acceptable from an ease to repair standpoint than if a wall had been demolished. It was a slightly different story with the building where kitchen goods and supplies were stored for the winter.

The bear had figured out how to get in, rummaged around and pushed almost everything he could get into and consume out the entrance. When McGregor and crew arrived in late spring with some snow still on the ground, they faced a pile of trash stacked high, spreading away from the shed's door.

The field season nevertheless proved to be a good one despite the inauspicious start. McGregor felt he had a good drill crew as well as some excellent geology students from the Colorado School of Mines he employed for the summer. He thought they acquitted themselves well and did an excellent job of compiling all the critical data.

In reflecting on his long, contentious fight with the National Park Service and Chuck Gilbert, McGregor speculated that the early history of greed and graft surrounding the coal leases given away in the early 1900s in the Wrangell-St. Elias Mountains by then-Interior Secretary Ballinger had prejudiced the Park Service against him and his partners. To McGregor it seemed as if the National Park Service viewed them as the reincarnation of J. P. Morgan and Samuel Guggenheim.

Gilbert dismisses this speculation. To Gilbert the record reflects extensive effort by the Park Service to try to work with McGregor, all to no avail because of McGregor's clinging to unsupported (in the Park Service's view) over-estimates of the value of the minerals locked in Orange Hill.

Asked what he thought had been the total outlay he and his partners had contributed over the years, McGregor said that as of January 31, 1977, when they entered into the agreement with U.S. Borax, the Venture had expended $1,222,755.42. At that time, the AJV interest in the venture was 40.41 percent. One of the properties McGregor contributed was the town site of Ellamar, which was built on patented mining claims that he also had purchased for $25,000. He later sold that site for $425,000 to secure additional funds to reinvest in continuing exploratory work.

During one interview, McGregor emphasized that neither he nor any of his partners, were oblivious to the beauties within the Wrangell-St. Elias. He said the mountains were incredible, the vistas from various points simply stunning. They fully understood why it would be included in the new national parks created by the Alaska lands legislation and why the Wrangell-St. Elias National Park would be as large as Switzerland.

McGregor said recently their big mistake was not filing a Mine Plan of Operation. Once the park and adjacent preserves were created, he and his partners accepted the act of Congress. They saw no reason to jump through the hoops of a phony exercise when realistically they "knew" they would never be allowed to operate a mine.

To this day, however, McGregor feels the old saying, "no good deed goes unpunished" applied to him and his partners both in the court of law, as well as the court of public opinion.

The Orange Hill property had a 1,700-foot airstrip on the gravel bar along side the Nabesna River. This "back country" strip provided access for hunters seeking trophy Dall Sheep which inhabited McGregor's property and the surrounding mountains. Use of the airstrip increased dramatically in 1978 as the drilling activities of Borax became known widely across mining circles.

The attention was enough to attract the interest of high profile environmental activists, such as the late folk singer, John Denver. Likewise, congressional delegations, including one led by Alaskan Senator Mike Gravel, flew in to inspect the drilling activities. Such high-profile attention didn't bode well for continued drilling activity at Orange Hill.

By the close of the 1980 field season, exploration coordinated at Orange Hill under McGregor's direction over a 13-year period had cost an estimated $1.5 million in 1970 dollars. Not a huge sum by some calculations, but real money to an "up by his own bootstraps" kind of guy, like McGregor.

When McGregor finally quit exploring and mapping Orange Hill, the proven reserves, as calculated by Borax at a grade of 0.2% copper equivalent (including molybdenum credits, but not including silver or gold) were 115.7 million tons averaging 0.308% Cu equivalent. At the then current metal prices the gross metal value of the proven reserves, according to McGregor, including copper, molybdenum and silver, was over $3 billion.

McGregor's number (and, Borax's, he says) was not validated by two separate valuations conducted for the Park Service, including one by a Spokane firm endorsed by McGregor himself. McGregor then had another private firm critique it.

At the outset of the passage of ANILCA, both McGregor's partnership and Borax believed that the intent of Congress was to allow the mining of the property. In 1985, however, the National Park Service was temporarily enjoined by a group of environmental organizations from approving any more mining plans of operation, and their outlook changed.

Both parties to the agreement read the writing on the wall, as did other property owners in the area. With no end in sight to the land moratorium put in place by then Interior Secretary Cecil D. Andrus, the parties concluded that the right to conduct mining within a park was no longer a realistic expectation. By mutual agreement, the Exploration Agreement and Option to Purchase was terminated. Under the circumstances, the Venture could not justify the continued cost of maintaining the unpatented claims, and therefore allowed those claims to lapse. Of course, the 100-plus patented claims remained.

Faced with the same decision, Kennecott Copper Co., in like manner, terminated its holding on the Bond Creek copper-molybdenum deposit located approximately four miles to the east of Orange Hill.

The joint venture lapsed into limbo awaiting the outcome of the Federal Environmental Impact Statement and the resolution of environmentalist lawsuits against the NPS.

A Record of Decision was then drawn up and initiated by the Park Service to address the matter of mine claims, both patented and unpatented. On August 21, 1990, the Wrangell-St. Elias National Park announced that the preferred action was to implement Alternative D in the FEIS: Acquire All Claims.

The Record of Decision cited, deliberately in McGregor's view, an incorrect estimate of the gross value of the mining claims in all of the WRST as between $13.5 million and $19.0 million. McGregor contends that his study was based in facts and in rational scientific analysis. Bottom line to McGregor and his partners: The ROD, in their view, was clearly not an accurate estimate of the mineral estate.

Gilbert points out that the values in the ROD were only meant to be estimates and that any proposed purchase of a mining claim would need to be preceded by completion of full appraisals.

On November 5, 1990, attorneys for McGregor submitted a Freedom of Information request to the NPS's Alaska Regional Director, asking for copies of all the information used by the NPS to arrive at the value of the patented claims at Orange Hill for the Record of Decision. The reply, dated December 5, 1990, enclosed comparable sales sheets, none of which, according to McGregor, was based on mineral estate values. Nor was the information specific to the Orange Hill. It did include a page entitled "Lode Values – WRST," which briefly described the significant mineral property holdings within the new national park.

The information did disclose that the Orange Hill property was the largest holding of unpatented mining claims (35% of the total unpatented claims) and the second largest of total claims, after Kennecott's long-held claims (representing 21% of the total unpatented and patented claims) in the park. The information also revealed that the development potential for Orange Hill was "High Future" potential.

This was according to the NPS's own disclosures, McGregor points out. But some ambiguity remained.

A cover letter included: "When the 1987 mineral estate value estimates were made, copper had traded at 60 to 80 cents per pound. This represents an increase of about 70 percent more than the increase in the cost of production."

In early April 1992, McGregor received a telephone call from Russell Lesko in the NPS Superintendent's office of WRST, inquiring whether McGregor and his partners would be interested in selling the property to the federal government. On April 6, 1992, McGregor wrote back to Superintendent Karen Wade to confirm their interest in selling the property. On April 30, 1992, not having received a reply from the superintendent, McGregor called Gilbert to discuss what could be done to move the acquisitions process ahead. The call was followed with a second letter to the superintendent on May 5, 1992. Gilbert says once again he did all that he could to get answers for McGregor's questions.

On May 10, 1992, McGregor contacted Norman Lee, chief appraiser of the Alaska Office of the NPS, and also wrote a letter to the NPS Regional Director on May 11, 1992. In both letters, he requested that the NPS carry out a mineral appraisal of Orange Hill, to determine both the surface and subsurface values. On behalf of the partnership, McGregor further offered to do whatever they could to cooperate and facilitate the appraisals.

At this point in the process, McGregor decided that he might need the support of the congressional delegations for Alaska and Washington. To that end, he sent copies of the NPS letters to Senators Ted Stevens and Frank Murkowski of Alaska, Senator Slade Gorton of Washington, Representative Don Young of

Alaska and Representative Sid Morrison of Washington, as well as his home district's representative, Speaker of the House Tom Foley.

McGregor felt the offices of Senators Stevens and Gorton were particularly helpful.

In one exchange of correspondence, Gorton wrote to Stevens requesting an answer to the question as to why funds were being appropriated only for acquisition of in-holdings and patented mine claims in the Kantishna area of the Denali National Park and Preserve. Senator Stevens, in his reply to Senator Gorton, argued that the NPS would not approve plans of operation to mine in the Denali National Park. The senator failed to understand that the same circumstances were true of WRST in-holders who were also being denied the right to explore, much less the right to mine, they claimed.

Finally, the WST Park Superintendent responded to McGregor's plea for action. In a letter dated June 19, 1992, she pointed out that, "Until money is appropriated for claim acquisition in WRST, we cannot proceed with the appraisal of your property." Superintendent Wade replied also, on June 18, stating that she had nothing to add to the comments of Chuck Gilbert.

On June 30, 1992, the partners asked Wade to clarify the terms of RS 2477, a recently passed state of Alaska bill governing their right to access their property.. She replied on July 29, 1992 that, "The NPS is not currently processing RS 2477 Assertions pending completion of internal procedures."

On August 17, 1992, the joint venture's management committee met to review the status of the property for the purpose of developing a strategy to compel the NPS to acquire the property as set forth in its own Record of Decision.

On December 8, 1992, Gilbert assured McGregor in a telephone conversation that the right of access across NPS lands was guaranteed with or without the assertion of RS 2477. McGregor claims this was one of several deliberately misleading statements Gilbert made. A legal analysis backs Gilbert's interpretation.

Regardless, on December 12, 1992, the Joint Venture submitted an application for certification of the trail into Orange Hill as a RS

2477 "right of way." The right-of-way for the Orange Hill trail was accepted by the Alaska State Department of Natural Resources on March 10, 1994. McGregor felt that the river itself as well as the air strip provided a guaranteed access, but once in production they would need a seven-mile road following the old trail that ran beside the river.

What McGregor did not see coming was that if he pursued the road, at least one solid bridge had to be built to ensure safe ingress and egress during high water run-off times. The initial estimated cost was $25 million.

At the August 1992 management committee meeting the partners settled on a strategy of trying to arrange a land exchange in 1993 with the Department of the Interior. The effort began with a letter on February 5, 1993, to Senator Stevens seeking his help. Stevens replied on February 23, 1993, and expressed appreciation for being kept informed on the Venture's current situation.

However, much to McGregor's disappointment, the senator said he could not get involved in negotiations regarding an exchange. A member of the senator's staff reported by telephone on February 25, 1993 that the NPS "resists the idea of exchanges." McGregor thought Senator Stevens clearly was not going to buck the NPS bias and in effect was lending support to the agency by his inaction to what McGregor saw as the Park Service's on-going strategy of stonewalling and delay.

On November 6, 1993, Alaska's junior senator, Frank Murkowski, chairman of the Subcommittee on Public Lands, National Parks and Forests of the Committee on Energy and Natural Resources, held a hearing in Anchorage at which McGregor presented a statement calling for fair compensation for the taking of their patented, valid property.

The combined efforts of the Alaska Congressional delegation, especially Senator Stevens, the owners, and their legal representatives, the Alaska Miners Association, the Department of the Interior, the National Park Service, and many others resulted in the enactment of section 120 of Public Law 105-83.

The law authorizes the legislative taking of mining claims in the Kantishna area of Denali National Park. If owners of claims consented in writing during a 90-day period ending February 12, 1998, title to their claims would pass to the USA on that date, and "just compensation" would be determined by the courts or by settlements.

With the interest being shown by Senator Murkowski, as well as other members of Congress, in the plight of the mineral in-holders in the Denali National Park, letters were sent to Senator Murkowski from Tom Henricksen, Project Manager at Orange Hill for Borax from 1979 through 1980 and from Jackie E. Stephens, Northwest District Geologist for Borax during the same period. Both expressed their strong views regarding the significance of the Orange Hill mineral resource, the importance of respecting private property, and concerns regarding uncompensated takings.

Two things brought McGregor and his partners out of the doldrums in early 1996.

First, McGregor hit upon the idea of approaching the leadership of the Native Regional Corporation in which the Orange Hill property lay. The 1971 Alaska Native Claims Settlement Act, besides allowing Native land selections and conveyances to go forward (primarily land adjacent to their villages), also established 13 Regional Native Corporations to handle business and assist in the distribution of the initial grant of substantial cash. ANCSA did *not* allow individual property selection and ownership – still a sore point even today with Alaska's Natives some 40 years after ANCSA's passage.

Some of these corporations did very well. They brought in outside advisors, were prudent in investing, were transparent and followed sound business practices and all the laws. One of the more successful was the Sealaska Corporation which operated in southeast Alaska and is primarily made up of members of the Tlingit and Haida Nations.

This corporation McGregor knew was and still is blessed with exceptional leadership, first from John Borbridge and then Byron Mallott, who has one of the most impressive resumes in Alaska. He has served as president of the powerful Alaska Federation of Natives, as President of the Sealaska Corporation, and later went on to serve as the executive director of the Alaska Permanent Fund. Today he is the lieutenant governor of Alaska.

The Alaska Permanent Fund was set up by former Governor Jay Hammond, who thought it would be wise to save a percentage of the trans-Alaska pipeline revenue and its oil throughput in a state savings account. Each year, a distribution drawn from just the interest accruing on that fund is paid out to every legal resident of Alaska. The success of this fund reinforces the message that wise and responsible development of a state's natural resources can, in fact, be accomplished. As the manager of this fund, Mallott's name was on the annual distribution check.

On November 4, 2014, Mallott was elected Lieutenant Governor on the fusion ticket headed by independent Bill Walker. Mallott had originally been the Democratic nominee for governor and considered the chief challenger to incumbent Governor Sean Parnell, but Walker proved increasingly attractive to Alaska's voters. When a poll showed that if Mallott joined Walker on his independent ticket, together that would create a head –to-head that the Walker/Mallott ticket would narrowly win, so he subsumed his ambitions and reached his understanding with Walker. They won.

The Orange Hill property is located within the area of another well-run native corporation called the Ahtna (ought-nah). McGregor encouraged Ahtna Corporation to organize claims held by Inspiration Mining Company that were contiguous with their claims. Basically, Inspiration conveyed the claims to Ahtna as a gift thinking that Ahtna would pursue development of the property which was an extension of the high-grade massive sulfide bearing unpatented claims within the Joint Venture's domain.

After a few years, Ahtna determined the holding cost was too great. This again tends to reinforce the appraisals ordered up by Gilbert which concluded the site is not an economically developable site. The result was McGregor encouraged Ahtna to hand off the unpatented claims to the University of Alaska-Fairbanks. A sale of the claims was ultimately made to the University.

The Joint Venture determined to do the same thing, and entered into negotiations. Their thought was to approach the University because they thought the UA-Fairbanks might have the political power to force the NPS to the table.

The partners offered to convey their ownership of the Orange Hill property to the university, subject to a retained interest by the partners in the net proceeds from the sale or exchange of the property. In a meeting in Fairbanks on July 30, 1996 between McGregor's attorneys and the university's, the concept was agreed to in principle.

Dames & Moore was hired to conduct an Environmental Site Assessment to quantify possible environmental liability. In a September 17, 1996 report, they concluded there was no significant environmental impairment.

Shortly thereafter, the university president resigned and the trustee with whom negotiations were being conducted was named head of the Selection Committee, bringing negotiations to a halt. During the period of limbo that followed, McGregor was approached by the NPS in a February 19, 1998 letter from WRST geologist Danny Rosenkrans asking if the Joint Venture was still interested in selling its patented mining claims as McGregor had mentioned six years earlier in a letter to the NPS.

The operative paragraph in the letter stated, "In 1992 you contacted the NPS and expressed an interest in selling your patented mining claims. At the time no acquisition funds were available. If you are still interested, please contact this office."

On March 10, 1998, McGregor responded, "Northwest Explorations is committed to proceed with a contractual relationship that precludes consideration of a sale of the Property to the National Park Service."

Hindsight is always 20/20, and in light of subsequent events, McGregor conceded later they should have explored this opening a little more diligently than they did.

In the meantime, negotiations with the University of Alaska remained in a state of limbo. When resumed, they raised the question of whether the university would have the right to sell mineral rights once acquired. In an effort to keep the negotiation on track, McGregor and his partners offered to change its proposed relationship. In lieu of a contribution of the property, they offered to name the university as its agent with the same sharing of net revenues as an incentive to gain the agreement of the NPS to proceed with a plan to acquire the property. Thus, they hoped to gain a clearly all-Alaskan partner.

In June of 1998 the director of the University Office of Land Management indicated to McGregor that there was concern about what the political tendencies of a new Board of Regents might be. It was thought that Governor Tony Knowles, who had been serving as Mayor of Anchorage before being elected to the governorship in 1994, was going to make some substantial changes on the board to put his stamp more clearly on it as he moved towards his 1998 re-election campaign.

McGregor was told there was a possibility that the university might not want to push for a sale of the Orange Hill property due to higher priorities. Concerns were raised about using the university's political capital to benefit an out-of-state partnership. The revelation of the uncertain compatibility of the university's objectives and those of the partners with regard to disposition of the property necessitated reconsideration of their action plan.

On July 10, 1998, at a partner's management committee meeting, McGregor and his partners unanimously agreed to withdraw both the offer to contribute the property to the university and the proposal to create an agency relationship with the university. Others might contend they acquiesced to the inevitable and decided to proactively frame the issues should there be any media interest, rather than react. There were no media inquiries.

In August of 1998, the Joint Venture learned that the NPS had closed on the purchase of the surface estate of a 1,000-acre parcel of the Kennecott property in the vicinity of McCarthy at a purchase price of $3.6 million. Initially, they thought the action indicated the initiation of a new policy for dealing with in-holders.

They later learned, however, from Kennecott's attorney that the negotiations had been in progress for eight years. During that period, the NPS claimed not to have the funds available for appraisals in the WRST, but they had in fact funded repeated appraisals related to the Kennecott acquisition, McGregor charged.

Gilbert said they had no funds for appraising or buying mining claims so at Kennecott they bought the historic surface estate and the company donated the mineral estate. He points out the statements are not inconsistent inasmuch as the master of the Senate appropriations process, Senator Stevens, directed acquisition funds be expended first for Denali in-holders.

Reluctantly, McGregor sent another letter to the WRST Superintendent requesting a clarification of NPS intentions regarding the Orange Hill property. The ensuing correspondence and telephone conversations held no surprises for McGregor inasmuch as it directed him to deal directly with Gilbert.

McGregor felt that Gilbert was playing the classic bureaucratic waiting game. Gilbert emphatically denies this, pointing out that Congress had not provided funds for purchases of mining claims in the Wrangell-St. Elias, even though the Park Service had requested them since the early 1990s.

In a letter of reply to the partners on November 5, 1998, Gilbert stated, "We remain interested in acquiring the Orange Hill Property and will be glad to arrange to have an appraisal done next field season." An authorization form, Owner's Permission To Inspect and Appraise, was enclosed with a request to review and sign. The letter directed McGregor to address further questions about appraisals for the mining claim acquisition program to NPS Regional Appraiser, Stuart Snyder.

McGregor says he called Snyder immediately to garner the information about the appraisal process the NPS would need. McGregor harbored the hope of coming to an understanding regarding the parameters of the appraisal and mutually to agree upon the selection of the appraiser. In a subsequent telephone discussion, McGregor said Snyder seemed amenable to a good working relationship. He also offered to inquire with other government agencies about mineral appraisers acceptable to the

NPS. Within 10 days, McGregor said Snyder delivered on his commitment and offered to the Joint Venture the name of an NPS-approved mineral appraiser.

McGregor then conducted his own independent research into the qualifications of several mineral appraisers, in addition to conducting due diligence on the recommended appraiser. On December 18, 1998, McGregor held a meeting with Snyder at his office in Seattle, at which time he indicated to Snyder that the Joint Venture approved the NPS' selection to perform the appraisal.

McGregor thought this was a good sign of possible cooperation but claims when he next talked with Snyder the cooperative demeanor suddenly changed. McGregor said Snyder transformed into a bureaucratic mode and informed him that WRST had a contractual relationship in place for all appraisals making it impossible to hire a specific appraiser for each appraisal.

Snyder, according to McGregor, claimed that the process of hiring an appraiser entailed advertising and the hiring of the appraiser from those responding to the advertisement. He said that, in any case, the decision regarding the final selection resided with Chuck Gilbert.

McGregor said he waited a couple of days and then called Gilbert, who confirmed Snyder's statement that all appraisers were currently under contract. Gilbert, according to McGregor, allowed it might be possible to subcontract the appraisal with the current contractor and said he would give the idea consideration. Gilbert insisted, however, that the current contractor be the appraiser.

McGregor saw this as more deliberate delay and questioned whether there would be enough time for anyone to get into the field before the short summer season was over.

McGregor said he remained concerned about the inability to arrive at an understanding regarding the parameters of the appraisal, but he believed that all that could be done had been done to prepare for a meaningful appraisal of the property. His partners authorized an application to proceed with an appraisal on February 18, 1999.

Three months later, in a telephone call on May 24, 1999, with Gilbert's assistant, Diane Wohlwend, McGregor said he learned that an appraiser to conduct the Orange Hill appraisals had not been hired. This fact was later confirmed in a telephone discussion with the appraisal team of Jim and Ellen Hodos of Onstream Resources Managers, Inc., who commented during a telephone conversation in mid June that they had yet to sign a contract for the appraisals they were about to perform.

Shortly after learning that the appraisal had not been contracted for, McGregor said he brought the appraisal contract opportunity to the attention of certified mineral appraiser Trevor Ellis. McGregor's earlier independent investigation had indicated Ellis was experienced and competent. Ellis acted upon the information and wrote to Snyder offering his services to the NPS and requested that he be given consideration should appraisal contracts be advertised. McGregor claims Ellis did not receive a timely acknowledgment of the receipt of his letter nor was he informed of the appraisals in the WRST for which contracts were being considered but not yet assigned.

Finally, in a June 10, 1999 letter, Gilbert confirmed "that we now have a mineral appraisal contract in place and an approved scope of work for the 1999 summer season appraisal field work. Your property has been included on the list for appraisal this summer." The Hodoses confirmed they had contracted for a field examination of the Orange Hill property to be carried out on July 10 and 11, 1999. McGregor made arrangements to accompany the Hodoses on the property examination.

On the morning of July 10, they all met at the Devils Mountain Lodge in the town of Nabesna, the closest point by road to Orange Hill. The Hodoses flew in by helicopter. Before proceeding to the property, McGregor gave the Hodoses a briefing on its geology.

McGregor claims the comprehensiveness of the geologic data and the magnitude of the reserve estimates was visibly troubling to the Hodoses. In fact, Mr. Hodos expressed doubt that the NPS would proceed with the appraisal. Asked why, McGregor said he was non-committal but reiterated his doubts about the NPS's willingness to proceed with a full appraisal that would include both surface and subsurface estimates.

Gilbert flatly disputes this charge and says unequivocally that the appraisal conducted for the Park Service on Orange Hill, as well as other properties in the WRST, included both the surface and subsurface values. He says, McGregor just plain did not like the results.

Following the geologic review at the lodge, the group flew by helicopter to the site and carried out a day-long examination. They met again the next day at the Devils Mountain Lodge to further discuss the geology and mineral reserves before flying to the property as a final orientation for the appraisers. Following the examination, a copy of the complete dataset was sent to the Hodos office.

Later, in September, McGregor called the Hodoses to inquire how the study was proceeding. He was informed that they did not have a contract to proceed with the appraisal. McGregor subsequently received a letter from Gilbert confirming the decision of the NPS to not finalize the appraisal that season.

Gilbert states that these contractors were reassigned to a very high priority project by the Department of Justice, and the appraisal of the Orange Hill property unavoidably had to be put on hold.


If this description of the back-and-forth sounds complex, consider this: It's a summary.

# 7

# Lawyers and Lobbyists

*Arigetch Peaks in the Gates of the Arctic. Photo by National Park Service.*

Faced with what the owners of the Orange Hill property believed to be a December 31, 1999, statute of limitations deadline to appeal the loss of their ability to develop the Orange Hill property and derive value from it, McGregor said the Joint Venture was left with no recourse other than to file a lawsuit.

Willa Perlmutte, their lead attorney in Washington, D.C. with the firm of Patton & Boggs, informed the Park Service that the partners needed to protect their right to pursue an inverse condemnation action by year-end unless the Park Service proceeded with its commitment to complete the previously agreed-upon appraisal in a timely manner.

McGregor said when he informed Gilbert that the partnership needed to proceed due to the statute of limitations, Gilbert said he knew nothing about such a deadline for filing a takings action.

On December 22, 1999, David Mayberry, the Patton & Boggs attorney in Anchorage, filed a complaint with the Federal District Court charging the National Park Service with "committing a compensable taking of its 18 patented and 99 unpatented mining claims when mining operations having environmental impact were prohibited in the Wrangell-St. Elias National Park." McGregor said that attached to the filing was an offer to withdraw the suit upon the agreement of the National Park Service to conduct the appraisal.

At this point, however, Gilbert already had agreed to conduct an appraisal and the timing seemed to be the only real disagreement.

By retaining Patton & Boggs, McGregor and his partners were opening another front in Washington, D.C., for besides being an excellent law firm it is also one of the nation's top lobbying firms.

McGregor knew that retaining a high profile law and lobbying firm such as Patton & Boggs would not be inexpensive, but he was shocked by the thousands of dollars they were charged monthly.

Around this time McGregor became acquainted with Eric Williams, a new employee in the Spokane office of the Gallatin Group. (The author was one of the founders of, but is not

currently associated with, the Gallatin Group.) A native of Montana
and a journalism graduate of the University of Montana, he became
attracted to the mining industry. Eventually, he formed a consulting
firm that specialized in working with mining companies.

Williams and McGregor both belonged to the Northwest Mining
Association, Williams active in the group's communications
committee and McGregor on the executive committee. At a meeting
one day McGregor was reciting his difficulties at Orange Hill.
Williams, knowing that Cecil Andrus was Gallatin's chief
"rainmaker," thought Andrus might be able to assist McGregor. He
set up a meeting for me with McGregor. After that meeting, I
persuaded Andrus to send a letter to National Park Service Director
Bob Stanton, who we had known when Andrus was Interior
secretary. The letter basically asked Stanton to order his
subordinates to proceed with the long-sought appraisal.

A few years later, I once again convinced the governor that he
should write then Interior Secretary Ken Salazar to direct the Park
Service to enter into a formal adjudication process equivalent to
binding arbitration. Andrus did sincerely want to see McGregor's
case brought to some kind of closure; but, sensing another side to
the story as well, he wrote a considerably toned-down letter.


Gilbert vigorously defends the work he and other NPS-Alaska
workers have done, and the contracts the NPS has let to conduct
appraisals. He believes he made every effort to obtain the highest
quality evaluation of the Orange Hill property.

Gilbert is a self-described "military brat," and says their family
moved all over when he was young. Thus, early on he developed a
sense of independence and self-reliance. He attended Jeb Stuart
High School in Falls Church, Virginia, but graduated from the San
Rafael Military Academy, near San Francisco. He then went on to
college and obtained his B.A. with a major in U.S. History from the
University of California at San Diego. Gilbert said he always had an
interest in the out-of-doors, and immensely enjoyed backpacking,
canoeing, skiing, as well as hunting and fishing. One of his favorite
haunts was the "back country" of Yosemite National Park. He and
his wife moved to Anchorage in 1974. It was then that he joined the

National Park Service. He started out as a GS-7 writer/editor working on Environmental Impact Statements (EIS). During the years leading up to the passage of ANILCA in 1980, he worked on the proposals for new national park units. In the early 1980s he moved into the planning section, devising plans for use and management of the newly established units. In 1986 he switched into the Land Resource Teams and became its manager in 1990.

At this writing Gilbert still is active and team captain of a group working in the Alaska Regional Office. Since joining that office he and his group have completed 224 transactions that have brought 64,758 acres back into public ownership at a price tag of $66,272,209 or a little more than a thousand dollars an acre.

Gilbert told me that while at times he could sense the unseen hand of Ted Stevens, as well as the "pressure" created by Andrus writing Salazar, not once did he really feel he was being asked to do something he did not feel comfortable doing.

He believes his work, particularly with regard to McGregor's Orange Hill site, will withstand any scrutiny and he most certainly does not believe the site is even close to being worth the $45 million price figure Fred Gibson said was the value of this property.

Andrus almost instantly saw that an unintentional consequence of fulfilling the mandate of section 17-d-2 had created an issue in search of a solution and he felt obligated to try to help get the appraisal process going or some sort of binding negotiations.

Earlier, when Andrus had written Stanton, much to Andrus' surprise, Stanton replied quickly indicating his determination to proceed with contesting McGregor's suit alleging a taking. Stanton refused to order an appraisal while the suit was pending.

McGregor believes Stanton was so quick to respond because he had learned who would be hearing their taking case. The judge selected to hear their suit was Alaska Federal District Court Judge John W. Sedwick, who was believed to have a bias on "takings cases."

A 1992 appointee by President George H.W. Bush, a graduate of Dartmouth and Harvard law, Judge Sedwick's decisions in previous cases had turned on the premise that, if a Mine Plan of Operation had not been submitted or had not been denied, a taking had not occurred.

Thus, the federal government's first move was a motion to dismiss the case because Northwest Explorations should have submitted a mine plan of operation for NPS to review. The Department of Justice (representing the National Park Service) also said that a mine plan of operation did not have to have an already completed and submitted appraisal. The filing of a taking was therefore premature and they considered the suit to be incomplete, arbitrary and not in conformity with the law.

Thus, the Federal Court could not address their cause of action because no harm had taken place. Therefore, the Justice attorney made a motion for summary judgment and dismissal.

The Department of Justice's argument prevailed and Judge Sedwick dismissed the suit on the grounds it was premature and not ripe. McGregor believes that it became the major obstacle in the taking not being compensated for in any way.

Not withstanding this major loss on their inverse condemnation suit, McGregor and his partners continued to press for an appraisal while at the same time focusing more of their efforts on the D.C. front to gain Congressional support for an appraisal and for acquisition funding for their in holding in the WRST.


Having already engaged the legal side of Patton & Boggs, McGregor now retained the lobbying side in early 2000 as Washington, D.C. based counsel, and the Joint Venture adopted a strategy aimed at obtaining a provision in the FY 2001 Appropriations Bill which specifically instructed the NPS to take action to acquire the Orange Hill Property at a purchase price that was objectively fair and equitable.

Gilbert had become a skillful manager of the various issues surrounding the compensation of in-holdings in Alaska. He wasn't particularly worried even with McGregor retaining Tommy Boggs' firm. Gilbert read the appropriations directive carefully and determined that the language in the appropriations act did not require anything that was not already required under federal law and policy – that when the federal government purchases property, it must be of fair and equitable value.

Boggs was the son of former House Majority Leader, Louisiana Congressman Hale Boggs, who died tragically in a plane crash in 1972 with Alaskan Congressman Nick Begich. Bogg's mother, Lindy, succeeded her husband and she held the seat for a number of years. His sister, Cokie Roberts, was for many years a fixture on public television. The entire family was well connected and influential to say the least.

McGregor recounts extensive negotiations with Gilbert in the latter half of 2000. The result was McGregor and his partners agreed to an appraisal of just the surface estate and the NPS obtained such an appraisal. Gilbert let McGregor know that the NPS had gone ahead with a "fair market" appraisal of the surface estate only.

McGregor expressed surprise at this bit of information and chose not to comment publicly. McGregor also disputed Gilbert's statement that he and his partners had been told and had approved of the surface estate only appraisal.

McGregor said no such approval had been given, but Gilbert points to records in his files substantiating that approval was given, that he had several conference calls with the three owners together in late winter of 2000-2001 and they agreed to an appraisal of the surface estate with the idea, similar to a park service transaction with Kennecott Corporation and other landowners, in which the surface estate was purchased by the Park Service and the mineral estate was donated (with applicable tax benefits).

In January 2001, when the appraisal was completed and approved, Gilbert says he called McGregor and the partners and said he would send it to them. They told him, however, that they did not want it sent to them or to be told what the concluded value was. Gilbert said he followed their wishes and did not send it out.

Seeking to break this latest impasse on the parameters of how an appraisal of both the surface estate and the mineral estate would be performed, the Boggs firm and others helped McGregor arrange a meeting with NPS Chief Appraiser Gerald Stoebig and Chief Realty Officer Eugene Repoff in Washington, D.C. on March 5, 2001.

In opening the meeting, McGregor's attorney referred to the language of the FY 2001 appropriations bill that instructed the National Park Service to set a "purchase price that is objectively fair and equitable." His counsel then asked for the NPS view of the term "fairness."

Repoff's response was that the basis for judging fairness with regard to Orange Hill, in the absence of any appraisals was an unknown. McGregor says Repoff told them that they had "never heard of basis for fairness," absent up-to-date appraisals. McGregor says that set a bleak tone for the rest of the meeting. Stoebig even expressed the opinion that the mineral rights had not been diminished by enclosure within the park, McGregor claims.

This issue of affixing a value to the Venture's in-holding was starting to emerge as the insurmountable obstacle.

McGregor steadfastly told me he and his partners had never given the Park Service a number, had never indicated there was a range they would consider and he had no idea why Gilbert and the Park Service would tell those that inquired that McGregor and his partners were asking too much.

When I asked Gilbert about this, he said without hesitation that the partners had informed the Park Service that they thought their in-holding was worth $45 million.

Did Gilbert have a written source for the $45 million number? Within an hour of my inquiry, Gilbert e-mailed a letter to me written in September of 2010 in which Fred Gibson, an attorney in Texas and the George Brown Family Trust's representative to the board of the Joint Venture, pointedly said the partners thought the site was worth $45 million. (The letter is included in the appendix.)

McGregor said that was a number fabricated by the Park Service.

In any event, following the Repoff meeting McGregor concluded further discussions with the NPS were totally useless. Clearly, he and the Park Service were not going to agree on the parameters of a fair appraisal. At the close of the meeting, Repoff stated the obvious: Without a mutual agreement on the parameters, the need for an appraisal was moot.

On recommendation of their legal counsel, however, McGregor then reversed his decision to reject the real estate appraisal of the surface estate only. Gilbert provided McGregor a copy of the appraisal. In reviewing the appraisal, he read that, on November 29, 2000, the NPS contracted for a "real estate" appraisal, which the record shows all the owners had agreed to.

McGregor said the appraisal inspection was conducted with a fly-over of the Orange Hill property on December 5, 2000, and the results were submitted on December 29, 2000. He further claimed the appraiser reported: "the fair market value of the fee simple estate, less the mineral estate, in the subject property, is: ONE HUNDRED FORTY-SIX THOUSAND DOLLARS ($146,000.)" The per-acre value of $401.87 was the lowest per acre value of all WRST appraisals with one known exception, a property described as "rocky talus slopes."

Discouraged but still determined to gain significant compensation, McGregor and his partners turned the focus of their efforts to seeking a renewal of congressional help to resolve the impasse. They thought it prudent to select another, additional legal and lobbying firm but one with more Republican affiliations (Tommy Boggs was a major player in Democratic politics.). This led McGregor to Birch, Horton, Bittner & Cherot, a firm with close ties to Alaska's senior senator, Ted Stevens, as well as an office in Anchorage.

McGregor later said in an interview that the Joint Venture was encouraged by the thought that, with a newly elected Republican administration (George W. Bush), dealing with the bureaucracy would be easier. However, the National Park Service stood its ground.

Gilbert sums up conditions as they stand at present:

"We were directed by Congress to work to acquire this property, which we did do, as diligently as we could—but we needed agreement on appraisal standards and instructions. The Northwest Joint Venture did not agree."

The lobbying effort had in fact obtained some specific language in the agency's appropriations thanks largely to the considerable efforts of McGregor's home district congressman, Representative George Nethercutt (himself a former Stevens staffer). Appropriations for the NPS to fund WRST property acquisitions were placed in three annual budgets, and language included which gave instructions to the NPS specifically to acquire the Orange Hill Property for a fair and just compensation. McGregor realized in his later years that the Joint Venture should have sought what is called a specific "earmark," which at that time was not nearly as notorious as Representative Don Young's $100 million dollar earmark for the infamous Bridge to Nowhere. But they did not.

When, in the closing sessions of Congress in December 2004, the FY 2005 Appropriations Bill passed as an omnibus bill, again with no earmark of funds for the acquisition of Orange Hill, McGregor and his partners had to conclude that Congress, like the National Park Service, put great stock in the fact that a U.S. Federal judge had already ruled that no "taking" had taken place. At this point, the Joint Venture had expended over $600,000 on the two D.C. lobbying and legal firms in their efforts to gain significant compensation of Orange Hill, with nothing of real substance to show.

To again try to resolve the impasse, there was another meeting with McGregor and his partners on June 13, 2006, with Marcia Blaszak, the new National Park Service Regional Director for Alaska.

At the meeting McGregor believed Blaszak committed the Service to do a full and complete appraisal that included both surface and subsurface values. Gilbert again says unequivocally that is exactly what they did.

Before a complete appraisal could be done, a professional characterization of the mineralization of the Orange Hill property and an analysis of its economic feasibility needed to be prepared. The NPS selected Aventurine Engineering of Spokane to do this work, based on Aventurine's experience in mining economics and its excellent reputation.

On April 22 Gilbert authorized the firm to do the work. Thus, it came about that McGregor provided Aventurine with a complete file of data on the property. McGregor accused Gilbert of sabotaging this evaluation of the Orange Hill property also.

The Aventurine report was finally completed in January of 2008. It concluded that the Orange Hill property was not economic to mine.

Some observers saw the conclusion of the mine feasibility study as a vindication for Gilbert. He politely turns such comments aside, saying that, "I wasn't vindicated. I didn't have a personal judgment to make. I just accepted the conclusions of the experts."

It might have ended there, but it did not.

McGregor commissioned a critique of the Aventurine Study by the Fairbanks, Alaska-based engineering firm, H2T Mine Engineering Services, LLP. He claims their review revealed that specific excessive and understated costs were in the net total amount of $189.1 million. Of great economic significance, the Aventurine study attributed no value to silver, thus disregarding the recoverable value of 10,924,725 ounces of silver with a gross value of $197 million at the silver price of $18.03 per ounce (at the time of the report). McGregor said he later learned that the devaluation of the silver resource had purposefully been ordered by the NPS.

In their May, 2009 report, H2T Engineering estimated the mineral estate value of the property at $43 million in terms of discounted cash flow (at a 5% discounted rate).

In an amended report, Aventurine addressed all the issues raised in the H2T critique and again concluded the property was not economic to mine.

In 2008 the Department of the Interior's Appraisal Services Directorate, the bureau responsible for obtaining all monetary valuations for the various bureaus of the department, contracted for an appraisal of fee simple interest (both surface values and mineral estate) of the Orange Hill property. Paul Meiling, a well-respected private appraiser from Utah, did the appraisal. His appraisal concluded a value of $290,000.

On December 16, 2009, the Joint Venture's counsel submitted a letter to the U.S. Department of the Interior, documenting alleged deficiencies in Interior's appraisal, noting that the Appraisal Services Directorate had failed to provide a fair mineral valuation and requesting that valuation be resolved through arbitration or mediation.

This solution was rejected in a letter to the partners on April, 27, 2010 from Ms. Helen Honse of the Appraisal Services Directorate. She categorically rejected the need for a mineral valuation because the thorough Aventurine report had already concluded that the Orange Hill property was not economic to mine.

The final offer from the NPS for Orange Hill then was $435,000.

Whether $290,000, $146,000 or $435,000, it was too far to bridge.

# 8

# To the rescue?

*Andrus in Alaska. Photo by National Park Service.*

When, on December 2, 1980, President Jimmy Carter signed into law the hallmark of his four-year administration, the Alaska lands legislation, he turned to his good friend and former gubernatorial colleague, Interior Secretary Cecil D. Andrus, and handed him the first signing pen. It was President Carter's way of acknowledging the critical role played by the former Idaho governor, that his leadership and teamwork were critical to the successful passage of this unprecedented law.

One would think Wallace McGregor might harbor resentment towards the architect of what he believes to be the uncompensated taking of his private property. To the contrary and to McGregor's surprise, Andrus has been the lone public figure who has sympathized with McGregor's plight. Andrus is a problem solver, and he takes on vexing problems because he firmly believes reasonable people can work together and find solutions, especially if when they disagree, they do so without being disagreeable.

Andrus understands and fully supports property rights, as does Chuck Gilbert, as do most Americans. While McGregor worked diligently to frame the issue as support for one's private property rights, Andrus always suspected the issue was really all about value and how much.

Nonetheless, he felt that something somewhere had to be awry, that it shouldn't take 40 years to bring about closure.

It is also true that Andrus is on record having expressed frustration at times with the growing perception that the National Park Service is becoming an elitist organization. Andrus knew that any organization, whether public or private, basically operates by public consent. Lose the public trust and one loses public support, and its credibility suffers.

Andrus considers the National Park Service to be filled with many fine, dedicated public servants. Chuck Gilbert is one of those. Andrus rarely forgets a name or a face, and easily recalled fishing with a much younger, relatively new employee of the NPS, during his July, 1978 tour with selected media of the candidate sites for possible inclusion in the Alaska lands legislation.

While Andrus has staunchly supported the need to compensate fairly in-holders who have property that was enclosed within any of the new National Parks, or expansion of an existing one, he fully understands it is a function of funds being available. He would be the first to tell you it is not his place to second guess a competent public servant like Gilbert.

McGregor may have put too much stock in Andrus' decision to accept a suggestion from John Katz to send a letter to Secretary Salazar suggesting utilization of the Alternative Dispute Resolution process. After Salazar looked into the matter and sided with the National Park Service, he wrote Andrus a polite explanatory note. Andrus accepted Salazar's explanation and let the matter drop, much to McGregor's disappointment.

In one of his last interviews with me, McGregor said he was most impressed by the "deft" touch Andrus displayed in his dealings with the former department he headed. For example, McGregor cited Andrus' letter of September 13, 2000, to then NPS Director Bob Stanton. Andrus, in classic make-lemonade-out-of-a-lemon mode, put a positive spin on Judge Sedwick's rejection of their lawsuit.

Six years later, McGregor asked if Governor Andrus might consider a note to Senator Stevens asking if an "earmark" might be available, secured and then directed to the National Park Service to get going on the appraisal. Though Andrus and Stevens had tenaciously fought during the debate surrounding the Alaska lands legislation, they held each other in high regard.

Though at the height of his political power, Stevens chose to take a pass, candidly conceding that "earmarks" were out of style and he was not about to stick his neck out. He suggested Andrus see if his friends in the Nature Conservancy might assist. The matter ended there.

This is being written in the spring of 2015.

35 years have gone by.

So much time has elapsed that if McGregor, or his heirs, or someone who might purchase the property from him, wanted to try to start a mine the process would have to begin at the beginning again—ironically with the filing of a Mine Plan of Operation.

Many questions remain unanswered, and probably will always remain so.

To bring some sort of closure to the saga of Wallace McGregor, I asked both him and Chuck Gilbert to answer in writing a few brief questions. The questions and answers follow.

Q and A with Chuck Gilbert. Answers were sent on March 3, 2015:

1) Why did the Office of the Secretary and the National Park Service reject former Interior Secretary Andrus' suggestion that the Alternative Dispute Resolution process (ADR) be adopted?

Answer: A June 22, 2010 letter from the office of the secretary to the owners of Orange Hill claims stated that ". . .formal arbitration has no precedent in this type of case." The letter went on to encourage further negotiation with the National Park Service for the sale of the claims. I believe that it was understood that a thorough and professional appraisal of the value of the subject claims had been obtained by the government, and good faith offers made by the government to purchase the claims and that negotiation was the appropriate method of proceeding, and that arbitration would be neither appropriate nor productive.

2) McGregor admits to some mistakes. Did the NPS make any and can they comment on them?

Answer: Everyone makes mistakes, but I can't think of any substantive NPS mistakes in this case.

3) To what extent did you field check McGregor's claims?

Answer: NPS personnel mapped the patented claims and some of the unpatented claims (Before the unpatented claims were dropped in the 1980s). When a mine feasibility study was contracted [for] by the National Park Service, Mr. McGregor was asked to provide all the data he had on the claims to the economic geologist conducting the study—which he apparently did. The data provided included reports on prior field work, core sampling and analysis of the claims. All that information was thoroughly reviewed. The fee appraiser, Paul Meiling, also visited the property twice.

4) McGregor claims you have never understood the legal definition of what constitutes a full-blown mineral survey.

Answer: This office, under my direction, has contracted for a number of mineral appraisals and those appraisals were reviewed and approved by federal review appraisers and mining economists. They were determined to meet applicable appraisal standards. In the Orange Hill case the NPS contracted for a thorough mine feasibility study by a respected mining engineer from Spokane, who the claim owners strongly endorsed. That study concluded that the Orange Hill claims were not economic to mine. The DoI Office of Mineral Evaluation, a unit of the Office of Valuation Services (not the NPS or my office), contracted for an appraisal of the claim. The contract appraisal evaluated the full fee value of the Orange Hill claims, including the mineral estate.

5) McGregor claims the number $45,000,000 has never been suggested by he and his partners—that is a number he claims the NPS came up with.

Answer: McGregor has made that statement many times in many letters. It is entirely untrue. We have two letters from the owners of the Orange Hill claims that state that the value of the claims is $45,000,000. (Gilbert provided a copy of a letter from Fred Gibson who represented the George Brown Trust's interests and was their designee to the board of Northwest Exploration. The letter, dated 9-22-2010, unequivocally stated the $45,000,000 figure.) The National Park Service had no part in coming up with such a value.

6) McGregor contends the assessment performed by the NPS contractor was nothing but a fly-over and that the economic viability number was on just the one-third of the property and should have included the other two thirds.

Answer: The appraiser visited the property twice. As far as evaluating the mineral value of the property, the appraiser relied upon the prior mine feasibility study obtained by the NPS, but he also consulted with other independent economic geologists on this matter. The property the appraisal addressed was just the patented mining claims. The associated unpatented claims had been abandoned by the owners in the 1980s, so the owners of the Orange Hill claims had no ownership interest in those unpatented claims at the time the appraisal was performed, so they were not addressed in the appraisal.

7) McGregor states "I am convinced that Chuck Gilbert took personal delight in screwing us and purposely made it impossible to come to an agreement on any terms. He preferred to keep us at bay." Care to comment?

Answer: Not true. On the contrary, I would have been very pleased to be able to conclude the purchase of this property, but the circumstances didn't allow that to happen. We tried very hard to get the best objective and professional assessment of mine feasibility and valuation of the Orange Hill property, so that we could make a credible, solid offer that would be fair to the owners and the U.S. taxpayers.

8) Why do you think Ted Stevens first sought to assist the Denali in-holders?

Answer: There were a number of active mines in Denali that were stopped in 1985 by a court injunction. Many of the miners were Alaskan residents and contacted Senator Stevens. In 1990, when it was determined to purchase mining claims in Denali National Park, Wrangell-St. Elias National Park and Yukon-Charley Rivers National Preserve, Congress appropriated funds for mining claim purchases, but only within Denali National Park. Congressional appropriations for mining claims purchases in Wrangell-St. Elias did not occur until the fall of 1998.

[Gilbert makes a subtle but important point here: Neither McGregor nor either of his partners in Northwest Explorations was a resident of Alaska.]

9) Do you have a ball park understanding of how much McGregor and his partners would have settled for? Do you think they were being greedy?

Answer: The only value we ever received from the owners was $45,000,000. I always assumed they would settle for less, but there was no indication from them as to what value they might accept. We made a "best and final offer" at 50% more than the appraised value, but that offer was rejected by the owners.

10) Did you have to answer to anyone else in the NPS on your land acquisition decisions?

Answer: Like all employees, I have a supervisor and other higher level managers. I briefed them and consulted with them on all major decisions.

11) Can you provide the number of transactions or purchases of in-holdings, the acreage and the cost you have overseen in Alaska in your current role?

Answer: Yes. 224 tracts comprising 64,758 acres at a cost of $66,272,209.

12) Did you ever feel any political pressure on you?

Answer: The Orange Hill case received a lot of high level attention. There were letters and inquiries from former Secretary Andrus and Senator Stevens and others and specific directions in a Congressional appropriations act. There was a high level of interest within the Department of the Interior. I can honestly say that I did not feel political pressure to reach a specific result. Given the high level of attention, I did try my best to make progress in the Orange Hill case, to follow the law, regulations and proper procedures and to treat everyone fairly.

13) What's the next step? Is there a next step?

Answer: The NPS is still interested in purchasing the Orange Hill claims. Given the time that's now passed since the completion of the mine feasibility study and the appraisal, those documents would need to be redone. Even if they are redone, it's unlikely the conclusions and the values would change substantially. I'm not optimistic at this point about being able to come to a mutually agreeable conclusion any time soon.

What follows is the Q and A with Wallace McGregor conducted on January 26, 2015:

1) Did you and your partners have legal counsel who advised you not to develop a mine plan of operation?

Answer: The first stage of decision making was in partnership with U.S. Borax under the assumption that, ultimately, logic would prevail and we would be allowed to mine. The environmentalists immediately clouded the issue with lawsuits. It was when the WRST Management Plan was published in 1986 stating that there would be no mining (Note: McGregor mis-states the plan) that the agreement with U.S. Borax was mutually terminated. We had no option but to accept the taking and thereafter sought only compensation on the basis of the fact that Congress had determined the highest and best use and that we would be compensated as provided by law.

2) If you did have legal counsel, what was it and did you all ignore it?

Answer: B & R had legal counsel and I drew on the counsel of Jerry Boyd with Paine Hamblen. We abided by the recommendation of counsel.

3) Did Brown & Root and the George Brown Trust simply give up on the project? If so, when and why?

Answer: As a management committee decision, it was decided unanimously by the committee members on March 1, 2012, that the impediments to resolving the taking were beyond our ability to achieve equitable compensation.

4) Why didn't you approach Senator Stevens much earlier?

Answer: We did, but he had political reasons to focus first on the Denali Park inholdings and never gave us the time of day. George Nethercutt was our principal means to gain traction in Congress.

5) Why do you think the National Park Service treated you as badly as you believe they did?

Answer: Simply the fact that the NPS management set the goal of refusing to make reasonable compensation for the mineral estate. I am convinced that Chuck Gilbert took personal delight in screwing us and purposely made it impossible to come to an agreement on any terms. He preferred to hold us at bay.

6) Were there others like you in a similar predicament?

Answer: The major companies like Kennecott simply bailed out on seeking to gain compensation for their scattered mineral prospects in the Park. Significantly, we were later to learn that while we were fighting to gain the conducting of a mineral appraisal, the NPS was carrying out an eight year "negotiation" with Kennecott to acquire its property in McCarthy that involved many repeated appraisals at the time they were claiming lack of funds for appraisals.

7) Did you ever consider approaching these other companies to form a coalition?

Answer: There were no other mining claim holdings of the magnitude of Orange Hill other than the Kennecott property. The NPS picked up the isolated mining claims for token amounts which were readily acceptable by the claimholders because at least they got something.

8) What was the price you paid for Orange Hill when you purchased it in 1968?

Answer: $25,000

9) What was the price you charged George Brown when he bought a third in 1970?

Answer: The venture was organized with $500,000 cash for a 51% to Brown et al and the contribution by the AJV Corporation (Wallace McGregor) of the Orange Hill property and other properties valued in total at $480,392 for a 49% interest. On the next go around of investments the AJV 49% interest was valued at $1,470,000.00 and the joint venture as a whole at $3,000,000.00.

10) What do you estimate the partnership's total outlay was in this entire venture?

Answer: As of January 31, 1977, when we'd entered into the agreement with US Borax, the Venture had expended $1,222,755.42. AJV's major contribution was the town site of Ellamar and its patented mining claims, which McGregor had purchased for $25,000. He later sold it for $425,000. (Extrapolating those numbers but also taking into account the lack of site activity, and then add the some $600,000 McGregor admits was spent on lobbying costs, a gut guess is around $2.5 million was spent by Northwest Explorations.).

11) What dollar price would you have settled for had the NPS made you an offer?

Answer: (McGregor gave a convoluted answer to this one based on present values of money, discounted values, cash portions, etc. The bottom line seems to be he thinks they would have settled for $10,000,000—still a number so far above the $456,000 offer from the NPS that one can see the chasm remains impossibly wide.).

McGregor's partners in 2013 began to signal they had had enough and were going to cut their losses by pulling out of the joint venture. His KBR partner assigned a new attorney to represent their interests. McGregor felt the attorney clearly had been given instructions to end their involvement and close it out on their books.

The representative of George R. Brown's family trust, Fred Gibson, also joined with the attorney and they began to push McGregor to give up and walk away.

That's not McGregor's nature, however. He had invested so much time, sweat and tears not to mention money that he simply could not walk away. What to do, though, became difficult. He listened to a proposal from a D.C. attorney who would take over the fight with no risk to McGregor and no further capital input in exchange for 33 percent of the return.

It sounded too good to be true and so he said no.

# 9

# The Four Horsemen

*Nabesna Road (National Park Service)*

When the Alaska lands legislation became law in December of 1980, most Alaskans had genuine doubts about the value of additional set-asides. Already the home to a combination of large national monuments, national wildlife refuges and national parks, most Alaskans were not thrilled at the creation of more.

They saw it largely as a needless lockup of natural resources and doubted tourist dollars could ever replace the lost revenue.

There were a few brave souls who spoke out forcefully in support, but they were badly outnumbered by the opponents. Supporters were confident, however, that fellow Alaskans would come to see the valuable potential in income from the many eco-tourists and other visitors from around the world.

At the bill signing ceremony, the leading House proponent, Arizona Representative Morris Udall, brought a chuckle from the crowd by telling an anecdote about a display at the Fairbanks Fair.

Four dummies in chairs were dressed up as Jimmy Carter, Cecil Andrus, Mo Udall and the Ayatollah Khomeini. For a buck one could throw three bottles at whichever figure they disliked the most. If the person hit the bull's eye, the dummy would be dropped into a large tub of ice water. Carter, Andrus and Udall were more "popular" than the Ayatollah, according to Udall.

By nature, Alaskans tend to be libertarian and deeply resent the overly heavy hand sometimes displayed by various branches of the nation's federal establishment, including the National Park Service.

For most Alaskans, though, just as for the many folks in the Lower 48, Park Rangers are considered positive figures who lead one on trail hikes besides skillfully handling disputes, clearing trails, or discussing the habits of the bears within the park.

The NPS also makes excellent use of part-time and summertime employees. Camp hosts are hired as are ticket takers at park entrances. They all radiate pride in their uniform and genuinely enjoy helping visitors.

Most Alaskans recognize the importance of politics, and that in a smaller state one can have more impact. Most Alaskans expect to know and have met the members of their congressional delegation and the statewide officeholders.

Alaskans know that they have a stake in the political game, and stand to benefit by participating. As pointed out earlier, on a per capita basis Alaskans are easily the biggest net gainers from the U.S. Treasury with the federal annual subsidy topping a billion dollars. Alaskans want the money, but like people everywhere, they don't like the strings that come with it.

Politics is also a "contact" sport and virtually no incumbent, no matter how well-entrenched, is ever safe from a primary challenge. Alaska has become such a Republican state that the Republican primary often determines the outcome. There is also a large element of the new "Tea Party" faction making its presence known.

Alaska has attracted its share of would be office-seekers who easily and often can be tagged as carpet-baggers.

Nonetheless, the political participation rate is high. Besides the two major political parties, Alaska also has a vigorous independent party, an active Libertarian party and even a few "greenies."

Despite policy differences on a number of fronts, Alaskans know resource conversion (mining and logging) means both direct and indirect jobs, as well as taxes, fees, and revenue to the state of Alaska.

Alaskans also have an innate understanding of how resource conversion is one of the best ways to bring new money into the market place. They adhere to the belief that resource conversion is the base of the economic pyramid. Other elements of the economy, such as recreation, as well as the information economy, they see as just moving around dollars created from resource conversion.

While the Alaska lands legislation will forever be considered the crowning conservation accomplishment of the Carter Administration, it was not by any means as comprehensive and inclusive as some of its strongest supporters believed it should be. It is an undeniable fact that Ted Stevens was a *master* of the legislative process. He skillfully used that knowledge to delay passage during the 1980 year.

Stevens had carefully cultivated Interior Committee chairman and Washington Senator Henry M. "Scoop" Jackson over a number of years. Stevens not only was incredibly knowledgeable about the Alaska land issue, he could be intimidating to those who couldn't see past the bluster. He was one of the few senators who knew what was in every Alaska lands bill. Unlike most senators, Stevens briefed his staff; the staff did not brief him.

The Alaska senator, having watched in 1978 a watered-downed House bill get reinvigorated on the House floor with a series of amendments sponsored by House Interior committee chair Representative Morris Udall of Arizona, with the assistance of Congressmen John Seiberling of Ohio and Phil Burton of California, as well as an incredibly well-organized grass-roots lobbying effort by the Alaska Coalition, knew what his first move was: He asked for and received a commitment from Jackson that there would be no conference committee to hash out differences between the House version and the Senate version.

In other words, he would massage the bill as much as possible and then it would be a take or leave it decision for the House side and the Alaska Coalition to make.

Stevens then had all summer to whittle away at the Administration/Coalition's bill being sponsored by Senator Paul Tsongas, which he proceeded to do. He successfully forced a series of generally weakening amendments on his committee colleagues that the Alaska Coalition often only heard about when Andrus would attend sessions and then report back to Coalition Chair Chuck Clusen.

The lead lobbyist for the Alaska Coalition, Doug Scott, would from time to time "draft" a supportive member of Congress, such as Oregon Congressman Jim Weaver, to attend the closed door negotiating sessions to find out what was going on and to shake things up.

Often it would serve to stall Stevens' compromising efforts somewhat for the senator would storm out of the sessions all red-faced and angry while Weaver would saunter out with a wry smile on his face.

One of the reasons Stevens held Andrus in high regard was that, like Stevens himself, Andrus did his homework. He did not just rely on memos from staff to tell him what was in a bill. He read bills himself and could grasp faster than most what the implications were for proposed changes.

Stevens also shrewdly played to the growing anti-government movement in the west symbolized best by the Sagebrush Rebellion. One of the principles within this movement was that of property and the belief states should be allowed to wrest federal property away, and manage it themselves. In addition, the Sagebrushers believed the federal property belonged to those who lived on or near it.

Their attitude was to hell with the city slicker in New York City and to those who believed this city dweller had as much right to the federal lands as those living on or near.

These libertarian, anti-government types to the core, found their hero that year in the personage of California Governor Ronald Reagan, who they blessed with the Republican nomination for president. Stevens knew that it would easy to fold the anti-d-2 message into this movement. Issues like usurpation of state's rights and the promulgation of "stupid" rules and regulations were perfect fits.

Andrus understood the external politics of all this better than most, which is why at the end of the day not only the Interior team, but the White House team and the Alaska Coalition all looked to him for timely leadership on both short-term and longer-term strategy.

Elsewhere I have described Andrus as the quarterback on the team that handled the last second winning drive with the equally valuable assistance from "slotback" Chuck Clusen, "halfback" Brock Evans, and "fullback" Doug Scott.

While there's no denying that there were hundreds if not thousands of people involved in achieving the goal of protecting huge swaths of Alaska for generations to come, neither is there any denial that success would not have happened if any of the four were missing or any of the first team.

Keeping with the football analogy, I've selected the other nine (including the punter and the field goal kicker) starters who were indispensable to the success of the legislation. The list is mine, admittedly arbitrary and it could be easily challenged by someone with more of an insider's knowledge:

#5. Laurance Rockefeller, the man who raised much of the money and personally paid for full page ads in the *Post* and the *Times* as well as direct mail. The guiding force in Americans for Alaska, the advertising arm of the Alaska Coalition, he often personally wrote copy that captivated the public and ensured solid voter responses in almost all congressional districts. He also often led visiting teams of Coalition partners in visits to Capitol Hill to lobby delegations at critical junctures.

#6. Guy Martin, key advisor to Andrus within Interior who discussed tactics and both short-term and long-term strategy, coordinated with the White House and other agencies and worked closely with the Alaska Coalition. As one of two Alaskans on the starting team, his knowledge both of Alaska and the players was indispensable.

#7. Cynthia Wilson, The other key adviser to Andrus. A former D.C. lobbyist with the National Audubon Society, her familiarity with Alaskan issues as well as the environmental groups and their leadership, enabled her to work well in a compatible way with a variety of folks, almost all of whom had healthy egos. Wilson had worked with Lady Bird Johnson and Liz Carpenter when she first came to D.C. Though she and Martin sometimes clashed over tactics and/or strategy, both had strong personalities but were loyal and usually could resolve their differences. Andrus would be the first to admit that they were indispensable to him and key parts of his success in leading the Administration's effort.

#8. Jim Free, Deputy Legal Counsel for the President; because he was in the White House, Free often acted like he was the lead for the administration rather than Andrus. He demanded anything and everything that had to do with Alaska come across his desk. He was smart enough to never test Andrus' special relationship with the president. He did bring to the table, however, a rare discipline and coordination among the various agency lobbyists.

#9. Rep. Morris Udall, congressman from Tucson, Arizona, and chair of the House Interior committee. Of all the congressional advocates, Udall was just a cut above. His use of self-deprecating humor, his ability to tell good stories, his folksy charm, added to his legislative skill, lulled many opponents into a false sense of security. Perhaps his finest hour came not in 1980 with the passage of the legislation, but in 1978, when, working closely with the Alaska Coalition's leadership (Clusen, Scott and Evans), Udall brought to the floor of the House amendment after amendment that restored to the House version of the Alaska lands bill many of the provisions that had been stripped out in committee. A superb tactician as well as a good fundraiser, he was an inspiration to most of the Alaska Coalition.

#10. Celia Hunter. President of the Alaska Conservation Society, Ms. Hunter was also a member of the Wilderness Society board of governors and interim director of the society for three years. As a resident of College, Alaska, she was often able to bridge gaps between Alaskan conservationists and the East Coast cast that dominated the nation's major environmental groups.

#11. Harry Crandell, the mentor for Chuck Clusen and the man on loan to Rep. Seiberling from Udall who sat through every minute of every negotiating session in both the House and Senate. Thus he knew more than anybody how much damage Stevens had done to the point where he almost killed the baby he had such a hand in creating.

#12. Rep. John Seiberling. Heir to a tire company, Seiberling could have lived a life of ease but instead plunged into public service. Though soft-spoken, the hearings his committee held around the country spoke loudly and did much to help put the Alaska lands issue at the forefront of the public mind and a measurement of the Administration's success or failure. A camera buff, he took some wonderful photographs while in Alaska.

#13. Senator Paul Tsongas was the long-sought Senate champion of an Alaska lands bill. Though a freshman senator, he was not intimidated by Stevens' bluster and posturing, did his homework, stayed close to the Coalition. Nonetheless there are folks even today who feel he constantly was out-maneuvered and taken to the cleaners by Stevens.

The final Senate bill was one that many in the Coalition felt was too compromised. Earlier, in July, 1980, the Senate floor debate and preliminary votes on amendments stunned Stevens. He realized that he did not even have a majority of his own party's caucus. Several critical test votes that would restore Coalition favored language to the bill were won going away by Alaska Coalition supporters, and consistently by margins of 2 to 1.

Stevens reached in his bag of tricks and thoroughly snarled things up, literally snatching away a smashing Coalition victory. By the time the Senate returned from its August vacation the bill was so watered down that the Alaska Coalition announced it would not support the measure.

A great end-game debate ensued that came dangerously close to splitting the Coalition into irreconcilable factions.

Harry Crandell, formerly of the Wilderness Society, but during much of the Alaska lands debate a key staff person with Representative Seiberling's office and far more influential than many public officials, was not a happy man in October of 1980. After carefully reviewing the Senate bill largely driven by Ted Stevens' obstinacy and his acumen, it looked to Crandell like a big piece of Swiss cheese. In other words he thought it was full of holes and he was disappointed.

After pondering the matter he decided the Coalition should not push the bird they had in hand. They should work on a newer, stronger bill in the new Congress. What made him and others think they could get a better deal from an Interior secretary like James Watt and a president named Ronald Reagan is hard to fathom.

Crandell in particular was unhappy that Stevens had been able to strip out the wilderness designation for much of the Arctic Wildlife Refuge, thus preserving the risk of exploratory drilling being sanctioned some day.

Stevens also took care of a large pulp mill in southeast Alaska near Admiralty Island. He wrote into the legislation a mandatory 400 million board-feet cut annually and a $40 million a year subsidy for 10 years for the Tongass National Forest. These were but two of a dozen plus occasions where Stevens was able to alter and weaken the bill.

Crandell almost succeeded doing in the greatest conservation bill in history. He did succeed in splitting the leadership within the board into two factions – one that wanted to wait and not endorse the bill. Then there were those who wanted to get on with the show.

Andrus, at this critical juncture stepped in and more or less ended the debate by stating unequivocally the bill was going to be signed and victory proclaimed. The quarterback who had led the team to the winning touchdown was not about to take the points off the scoreboard.

Thirty-five years later I put several questions to the "backfield." The most critical regarded whether they thought, after having had 35 years to ponder it, Harry Crandell was correct? Or were the others correct to take the half loaf and proclaim victory?

Brock Evans, now retired and living in Washington, D.C., said he disagreed with Crandell. In fact Evans questioned whether Crandell really said such a thing. "If he really said that, sounds typical of what so many of our hardworking people usually say after a campaign," he wrote to me.

Evans said he thought all coalitions like the Alaska Coalition "start out with high hopes and great ambitions . . . . . then, after a few years' combat with a still powerful "other side" comes the final bill, riddled with compromises.

Evans recalled trying to cheer up Doug Scott at the 1980 office victory party following the bill signing. Scott, at the time, was especially upset at what Senator Stevens had been able to do with the Tongass National Forest, including a mandatory minimum 400 million board-feet cut annually to supply an aging pulp and paper mill and an annual, 10-year $40 million cash subsidy.

Ten years down the road, though, Evans points out that they were largely able to correct the mistakes by pushing through Congress the Tongass Timber Reform Act.

He also saw Crandell's reaction as fairly typical of one caught up in the day to day back and forth that becomes the sausage of legislation.

Evans wrote me, "Maybe I have been around D.C. too long, but even then the achievement of 80 to 100 million more acres of protected land designations forever, against the adamant opposition of Ted Stevens? I think that is quite an achievement and it looks better and better each passing day."

"Sure, we all wish it could have been more then; but altogether, even then, it was far far more than any of us had ever achieved in the Lower 48 states," Evans stated.

It is important to understand that the debate on whether to sign the Senate version began even before the November presidential election.

The National Parks and Conservation Association, the Department of the Interior, the National Audubon Society and the National Wildlife Federation all wanted to sign the Senate bill pronto.

Clusen himself wasn't sure but he was working hard to keep the coalition together. Some of the key members of his board including the representative from the Sierra Club, the Wilderness Society, the Southeast Alaska Conservation Coalition and the NRDC wanted to use the time between passage of the bill and the election to try to make changes but Stevens maintained his take it or leave it posture.

At the end of the day only the Southeast Alaska Conservation Coalition stood for rejecting the bill and trying for a better one down the road.

Thirty-five years later Evans is more certain than ever that they did the right thing in not waiting and trying for a better bill with Reagan in the White House and James Watt at Interior.

Evans had this to say: "I would not have waited. The future is always uncertain, and there was more opposition out there than just

Reagan and Watt (although that, all together was eight long years, remember).

"No – far better to seize the moment – and the chance – when we, our community was united as never before (or, since); and we had the public with us, and a whole congressional plan all laid out. If we had waited, John Sieberling would likely have been gone; many thousands of acres would have been plundered or committed to the same. We would have been less united; we would still have a Republican presidency (until 1992); things never stay the same, the politics rarely get better, and hindsight is always 20-20."

Asked if there was anything else he felt Andrus could have done to further the cause, Evans said perhaps Andrus could have fought harder for more protection for the Tongass and less access to the new parks and refuges, but he realized he was seeking the perfect and he could not let that be the enemy of the good.

He concluded his note to me with this thought:

"We are most successful when we sense that now is the time, and we reach out to seize the moment. Such is life, is it not? It is not a perfect world, so we always have to fight (hard) for every acre we get."

Of the three key leaders of the Coalition, Doug Scott probably sympathized the most with Harry Crandell's views. As the lead lobbyist and the one who organized much of the grass roots, Scott knew how hard the team of 20 lobbyists he had brought together had worked to restore much of what had been stripped out of H.R. 39 by winning votes on the House floor in 1978 and again in 1979. When Stevens and Jackson saw the same scenario unfolding in 1980 on the Senate floor, they "iced" the vehicle and Stevens invoked his agreement with Jackson. There would be no conference committee, just the Senate Interior committee's version as reworked by Stevens.

As disappointed as Scott was with the final compromised bill, though, even he conceded that in the final analysis with a Reagan presidential win looking more and more likely "we had to accept a Senate bill that was better than before our House victories, but still weak and inadequate in many ways – notably in the mandated timber harvest and minimal wilderness on the Tongass National Forest in the southeast of Alaska."

Thirty-five years later, Scott added this: "Harry was just too damned close to this and was aware of every evil comma and word that got changed. This doubtless arose in good part from the fact that unlike 1978, in the spring of 1979 we had the Udall/Seiberling bill hijacked by the bad guys. We had to go to the House floor (as they did in 1978) with the bad guys' version and, in a series of overwhelming votes, restore the stronger provisions.

"To see those then whittled down by the Senate was dispiriting to all. Unlike the rest of us, Harry Crandell was in the room for most of the long, long Senate/House negotiating sessions," Scott wrote in an e-mail.

With 20/20 hindsight, Scott said he would have recruited then Maryland congresswoman Barbara Mikulski to sit in those negotiating sessions between the two Interior committees. With a solid reputation for hard work a well as being tough and pugnacious, Mikulski no doubt might have fared better than Congressmen Udall and Seiberling. Though Scott dearly loved the both of them, as he said, they were both just "too nice."

To his credit, Scott also readily admits he was wrong in his initial assessment of Cecil Andrus. Scott felt that any successful western governor almost by definition had to have made serious compromises with the timber, mining and grazing interests in their state. In his mind this disqualified any western governor from holding the post of Interior Secretary. Though aware that Andrus had won his initial term in 1970 in part because of his daring opposition to a molybdenum mine in the White Clouds that in his mind still did not make him pure enough.

Scott even testified to his reservations before the Interior committee hearing on Andrus' nomination, something Andrus forgave but has never forgotten.

Even more surprising was that Scott was able to get Evans to join in expressing their reservations and stating a preference for Congresswoman Patsy Mink from Hawaii to be the Interior secretary.

Thirty-five years later both testify that Andrus was the right Interior secretary in the right place at the right time with the right skills to lead the team to the touchdown. They as well as Chuck Clusen have come to recognize that without Andrus' leadership there probably would have been no Alaskan lands legislation.

In particular in the end-game, Andrus never wavered in his stance that the Senate bill was historic and they were going to accept. The Andrus favorite expression recurs here: "Pigs get fat, but hogs get slaughtered."

For his part, Andrus has always recognized that without the Coalition's exceptional ground support—especially the phone bank that could generate thousands of cards and calls almost instantly in support of Scott's superbly organized lobbying the halls effort—the Administration never would have gotten any bill through the Congress.

While Andrus, in my view, was the quarterback who could call his own plays, by no means was he the only "signal-caller." There truly was a well-coordinated team approach between the advocacy groups and the Carter Administration and the credit for the success of both the external and internal coordinated communications goes in large part the critical role Chuck Clusen played as the Coalition chair.

Blessed with patience and grit, as well as an ability to listen, learn and observe, Clusen was also the right person in the right place at the right time with the right set of skills. He had an uncanny ability to deal with strong egos and personalities and to keep everyone focused on what the goal was that brought 55 disparate groups together in a one of a kind coalition the conservation community had never before seen and probably will never see again.

To Clusen fell the thankless task of keeping everyone on task. He had to be up on all the details every day, for "the devil is in the details." To Clusen fell the challenge of raising the funds to keep the effort going and to work with his friend Larry Rockefeller, who was personally writing and financing excellent full-page ads. Clusen was the one who had to smooth over the rough edges of some of the team, and still keep the smooth machine running.

Holding the coalition together in the last critical days may have just been another day at the office for him. Nonetheless, the diplomacy, finesse and skills he displayed then had to be one of his finest moments.

Making it especially challenging for Clusen was his deep and abiding respect for Harry Crandell. He considered Crandell to be both the mother of the Alaska lands legislation and of the Alaska Coalition.

Clusen wrote this about Crandell: "He constantly warned me about potential problems and presented original creative strategies. He was a mastermind. He knew that going to implementation of the Senate bill and its language would lead to many problems. And it has.

"I only point out the problems of the use of snow machines and predator control in Alaskan National Parks and Preserves. If President Carter had won and Secretary Andrus' team had done the implementation, we would have a much stronger system of protection on the public lands in Alaska today. Instead we got James Watt."

Clearly, sincere and generous praise from Clusen. What he does not know, and had no way really of knowing, was that at the very beginning of his tenure at Interior, Andrus told those that had come with him from Idaho to plan on his being Interior secretary for just one term . Then, he said, he was returning to Idaho and we all should plan accordingly.

Notwithstanding that fact, Clusen's statement is essentially on the mark.


Call it fate; call it serendipity; call it pure coincidence but the incontestable truth is all four of these players were irreplaceable. If anyone of the four had not been drawn into this epic fray, there would not have been any Alaska Lands legislation. The same could probably be said of the rest of the "starters"also:  Guy Martin, Cynthia Wilson, Laurance Rockefeller, Mo Udall, John Seiberling, Jim Free, Harry Crandell, Celia Hunter and Paul Tsongas.

Scott, Evans and Clusen all had several things in common
besides being intelligent, hard-working and dedicated to the cause
of environmental protection. All worked for the Sierra Club, and
Clusen and Scott attended the University of Michigan together.

Scott, who was born in Vancouver, Washington, and raised in
Portland, started his college career at Willamette University in
Salem, then switched to the University of Washington before
heading for Ann Arbor to attend the University of Michigan from
whom he obtained his B.A. in Forestry.

Scott then did some graduate work but he most enjoyed a job
he had in Washington, D.C., during the summer of 1968 in large
part because he met an equally dedicated environmentalist named
Chuck Clusen, who was headed to Ann Arbor to obtain his B.S. in
Conservation. Thus, they ended up rooming together one year.

Brock Evans was the oldest of the trio. He graduated with
honors from Princeton in the late 1950s, then joined the U.S.
Marine Corps, before deciding to pursue a law degree at the
University of Michigan.

Though all three share the University of Michigan in their
educational backgrounds, Evans attended the law school from
1960 to 1963 – a few years before Clusen and Evans were
students there. Given the rivalry between Ohio State (located in
Columbus, Ohio, where Evans was born and raised) and the
University of Michigan, one wonders if he ever dared return
home. Evans is a bit of a contrarian though, the wild salmon that
swims against the strongest part of a stream's current to prove
he's tougher than most. Lord knows what might have transpired
had the three known each other back in the early 60's, before the
word environmentalist had even been coined.

In October of 1979, Secretary Andrus flew to San Francisco to
deliver the dinner remarks at the Sierra Club's annual High Sierra
Dinner. He knew he was there to encourage the some 800
attendees to stay the course, that the goal line was within sight
and the long-sought protection of entire ecosystems which had
barely been touched by man was about to be achieved.

It was an electric moment and a lovefest. When introduced
and before having said a word, the crowd stood and roared its

approval with a spontaneous, sustained five minute ovation. The crowd knew the architect and engineer of the greatest conservation action in the history of America was standing in front of them.

Some in the audience might have pondered the irony of the moment inasmuch as their champion was not by any stretch of the imagination a "tree-huggin', posey-sniffin' preservationist." He called himself a "common sense conservationist," one who knew there was real value in protecting the environment for future generations to enjoy, but one who also had governed Idaho successfully following his mantra: "First, you have to make a living, then you have to have a living worthwhile."

Some may even have known that Andrus was a convert to the cause; that in his youth as a lumberjack and gyppo logger Andrus had once skid logs down a stream bed – a practice he ceased rather quickly for as a sportsman and a fisherman he quickly saw the damage being done to the watershed and the fishery.

Few in attendance knew that the tall, already balding, impeccably dressed gentleman with the fabulous smile and the quick wit was not an Ivy-League trained lawyer. Rather, he was truly a self-educated, lunch-bucket carrying Democrat from the woods of north Idaho.

Andrus, though not a great orator, delivered a great speech that night. He has a speaking style that always connects with his audience and conveys his message. He has a way with words that leaves what he says lingering in one's mind. He seldom reads from a text. He takes a text prepared for him and "Andrucizes" it. He mixes and matches while speaking, picking out a paragraph or a phrase and then puts it in his own words.

This particular evening he drilled down on one of the Alaska Coalition's favorite slogans: Alaska – the Last Chance to Do It Right the First Time. He described his own thoughts and feelings while leading some of the nation's best reporters on a tour of the d-2 lands the summer before and viewing the vast, migrating Porcupine caribou herd, the beauty of the Brooks Range and the grandeur of the Arigatch Peaks.

He concluded by painting with words a mental map of America, and then took the audience, now putty in his hand, on a trip starting on the east coast down to the Gulf of Mexico, then up the west coast to Alaska and on around Alaska to the Arctic Wildlife Refuge. His point was the oil industry could drill for oil in all of these places, but that there was one area left where they could not go, could not explore, that would remain inviolate and protected by wilderness designation.

"They can drill here, here, and here," he said, pointing to areas on the mental map, "but not there, not now, not ever." He sat down and for a few brief moments his audience sat mute before erupting with another roar and even longer sustained applause.

There wasn't a person in the audience that night that left that dinner not knowing that there was going to be an Alaska lands bill before the end of 1980. Like Joe Namath guaranteeing the New York Jets would win Super Bowl III over the then Baltimore Colts, the Sierra Club members heard the quarterback provide the inspiration that would roll over anything in its way.

From the day he left Plains following his meeting with President-elect Carter, who charged him with delivering on the president's commitment to the environmental community, Andrus never lost sight of the goal. As he would say, he kept his eye on the rabbit. In this case it should be amended to read he kept his eye on the caribou. His unique ability to look over the horizon and correctly guess that ultimately President Carter would have to use the Antiquities Act to force a solution and keep the Alaskan delegation at the table was especially critical to success. That he was the first to broach the probable need while on his fly fishing trip on Idaho's Middle Fork in the late summer of 1978 speaks for itself.

President Carter of course deserves ultimate credit. And yes, success has a thousand fathers and mothers, including hundreds of staff from the Interior department and other agencies, but most will agree that the four horses were Andrus, Clusen, Evans and Scott, along with the other "starters."

A grateful nation will eternally be in their debt.

# Acknowledgments

Over the years I've known and worked with many folks in the National Park Service and found virtually all of them good, reasonable people to be with and to work with. I think of people like Roger Contor, the fine chief ranger in the Olympic National Park, or Russ Dickenson, who Andrus made chief of the NPS, or Dave McCraney, an aide to John Hough in the Secretary's western field office on loan from the National Park Service.

Wallace McGregor chose to frame his argument in terms of a constitutional right denied. Once McGregor recognized that I was not writing the story the way he wanted it written, we came to a parting of the ways. I do want to thank him, however, for sharing his time, his thoughts and perspective, and his files during the period when we were both active on the project.

I owe Chuck Gilbert a special debt of gratitude for patiently working through all the charges and details of a complex story.

Much of this book is a memoir recounting my experiences with Governor Andrus and the passage of the legislation from the unique vantage point I occupied. I hope it provides future readers, students, teachers and historians with an insight into the role he played.

Laced throughout are anecdotes that add color to these stories. It is by no means meant to be a definitive, academic history subjected to peer review by university types steeped in history who seek more detail than often is necessary to interpret what transpired in the past. A truly definitive, readable history is yet to be written but one is in the process of being produced by Douglas Brinkley. It will comprise the third volume of the definitive history of the Alaska lands issue he has been working on for some time.

His second volume, entitled *The Quiet World*, is true tour de force which helped provide much good background. Another superb "background" book was that written by Mary Clay Berry, which helped to provide essential information salted throughout this book. Her book, entitled *The Alaska Pipeline: The Politics of Oil and Native Land Claims*, is one of the finest one can read and I believe is the definitive work on passage of both the Native Land Claims bill in 1971 and the trans-Alaska pipeline legislation in 1973. Some may legitimately argue that the two books written by Don Craig Mitchell, a former attorney for the Alaskan Federation of Natives (AFN), and entitled *Take My Land, Take My Life* and *American Promise*, are just as good.

I owe a special thanks to Cynthia Wilson who headed up the Interior Internal Taskforce on the Alaska Lands established by Secretary Andrus. She graciously put together the invaluable timeline of key dates. I had hoped she would join with me and this book would have had co-authors. Her candid assessment of the original text's shortcomings proved invaluable in producing a more balanced account.

She is one of several people whose knowledge of the details easily exceeded mine. Nonetheless, she agreed to review and critique this effort and her insight was most helpful, as was Andrus' former Assistant Secretary for Land and Water, Guy Martin. A former legislative director for Congressman Nick Begich, as well as a former Alaska Commissioner for Natural Resources under Governor Hammond, Martin's insights were valued and important to the book's final form.

Others who provided guidance, insight, wisdom and solid editing include my long-time friend, chief editor and critic, Jay Shelledy, the former editor of the *Salt Lake Tribune*, who currently is teaching journalism at Louisiana State University. He also edited my first two books making them better products in the process. Thanks also goes to our mutual friend, A.L. "Butch" Alford, Jr., the publisher emeritus of the *Lewiston Tribune* and a long-time friend who graciously read every word and provided me with some excellent edits. Others who graciously read initial drafts and provided solid suggestions include Gary Catron, the aforementioned Ms. Berry and my fine deputy at Interior, Harmon Kallman. My thanks to all for at our age our choices on how to spend our dwindling time become ever so reflective of who and what we really value.

My publisher at Ridenbaugh Books, Randy Stapilus, deserves special thanks both for solid editing suggestions and his talent for great layout of my books. Even his selection of the right font that often enables one to more easily read my books is uncanny. I also thank his managing editor, Linda Watkins, for her always careful editing of manuscripts.

I would be remiss in not mentioning my continuing debt of gratitude to my column publisher, Dan Hammes, at the *St. Maries Gazette-Record*, which I consider to be my flagship carrier. His support as well as help in terms of time, resources and personnel has been unflagging throughout the process of producing the three books. I owe him a debt that I probably can never repay but he will always have my thanks, appreciation and friendship.

It goes without saying that I owe a continuing deep debt of gratitude to my former boss, the great and good former four-term governor of Idaho and Carter's Interior Secretary, Cecil D. Andrus. This book grew out of my belief that his key role in garnering passage of the historic Alaska lands legislation has never received its proper due.

As usual, he was most generous with his time in answering questions, checking through files or bringing his excellent memory to bear and correcting my increasingly faulty memory.

Last, but by no means least, and as always, I must thank my better half, my wife, Marcia, who is my best editor as well as best friend. Her incredible patience with me and some of my foibles goes truly above and beyond. It reflects our deep devotion and love for each other, though I feel I am a most unworthy recipient.

I trust those that read this account will have found it worth their time.

*Chris Carlson*
*Medimont, Idaho*
*June 6, 2015*

# Correspondence

*Letter #1: Fred Gibson to Charles Gilbert, 9/22/2010*

## GRBP
THE GEORGE R. BROWN PARTNERSHIP, L.P.

4700 FIRST CITY TOWER  •  1001 FANNIN  •  HOUSTON, TX 77002-6792  •  TELEPHONE: (713) 652-4901

September 22, 2010

Charles M. Gilbert
Chief, Land Resources Program Center
United States Department of the Interior
National Parks Service
Alaska Region
240 West 5th Avenue, Room 114
Anchorage, AK 99501

Dear Mr. Gilbert:

I am in receipt of your letter of September 9, 2010. The members of the Management Committee join me in expressing thanks for your offer to purchase the Orange Hill Patented Mineral Claims. We fully agree with you that time is of the essence to bring this process to a conclusion and we share your goal to have the property conveyed to the National Park Service.

As we discussed, the evaluation of a potential mining operation is a complex process that can result in significantly different answers depending on the assumptions made, the methodology involved and operational understanding. We envision a successful mining operation at Orange Hill and consequently view the value of the mineral estate to more properly represent the appraised value. Our best estimate remains a value of $45,000,000 in 2009 dollars using the discounted cash flow method.

It is clear that our individual evaluations have arrived at different conclusions. However, we are willing to work with the National Park Service to arrive at a mutually agreeable value by means of dispute resolution as provided by law and propose that we embark on that process. We are certain that such negotiations carried out in good faith can achieve the mutually desired goal of conveying the mineral property to the National Park Service as envisioned by Congress in creating the Wrangell-St. Elias National Park and Preserve in 1980.

Sincerely,

THE GEORGE R BROWN PARTNERSHIP LP

*Fred Gibson*

Fred Gibson
President

# Letter #2: Ken Salazar to Cecil D. Andrus, 2/15/2012

THE SECRETARY OF THE INTERIOR
WASHINGTON

FEB 1 5 2012

Mr. Cecil D. Andrus
1280 Candleridge Drive
Boise, Idaho 83712

Dear Mr. Andrus:

Thank you for your letter of September 19, 2011, regarding a 363-acre block of patented mining claims located in the Wrangell-St. Elias National Park and Preserve. The property is owned by Northwest Explorations Joint Venture and is generally referred to as the Orange Hill claims.

As a former Secretary of the Interior, you will appreciate that issues that seem simple on their face often have a significant history and are very complex. To make sure I understood the issue raised in your letter and those by the claim owners, I asked for a history of the issues involved. That history is enclosed.

The major issue is the vast difference in valuation between claim owners and the valuation done after an extensive appraisal process, including a mine feasibility study done by a firm the owners recommended. The Department of the Interior does not believe this case is suitable for an administrative dispute resolution given these vast differences. In addition, we are not in a position to commit to a process that will bind the National Parks Service to future payments without the consent of Congress.

Please let me know if you have further questions or additional information regarding this matter.

Sincerely,

Ken Salazar

Ken Salazar

Enclosure

263

# Letter #3: Cecil D. Andrus to Senator Ted Stevens, 2/13/2006

CECIL D. ANDRUS

February 13, 2006

Senator Ted Stevens
United States Senate
522 Hart Building
Washington, D.C. 20510-0201

Dear Senator:

As one of the few people remaining who were instrumental in the passage of ANILCA, I am writing to you concerning the Orange Hill property in the Wrangell-St. Elias property with which both of us are familiar, to request that action finally be taken to acquire the property as set forth in the WRST Record of Decision, published in August, 1990.

This is not the first time that I have deemed it appropriate to urge acquisition of this very important property in order to fulfill the promise of ANILCA. In 1993, I wrote to the National Park Service Director, Roger Stanton, urging completion of a long overdue mineral appraisal of the property, an appraisal, counted my information on hand that indicated major, potentially exploitable mineral reserves and also because of my strongly-held and publicized views that the greater conservation value of the area dictated that the deposit should not be allowed to be developed. In a letter to the owners, dated August 11, 2000, Director Stanton assured me that a mineral appraisal of the property would be initiated by October 1st of that year.

Now, six years later, I read in a recent issue of the Alaska Miner that the Orange Hill property remains not only without an appraisal for its mineral value, but the property has not, as of this date, been acquired. I am concerned that exploration of the mineral deposits of copper, molybdenum, and precious metals could, at current metal prices, be an economically viable option. I find such a prospect incompatible with the purpose of the Park.

It is remarkable that, to the benefit of conservation and in keeping with the essential purpose of ANILCA, the owners have, as of this date, refrained from acting in their own self interest by selling the property. The owners have indicated to me that, at some point, they will act in their own best interest by

(continued)

capitalizing on the increasing opportunities being presented t
sell the property for a private hunting and recreational lodge
Such a sale would be inimical to the best interest of the
National Park Service and to the protection of intact wilderne
ecosystems.

Surely common ground can be found in negotiations with th
owners to arrive at a fair purchase/contribution agreement, on
that would place the property under the control of the Nationa
Park Service. It is for these reasons that I urge attention b
turned to negotiations for the acquisition of the Orange Hill
patented mining claims without delay.

Closure on the Orange Hill property acquisition will serve
crucial purpose of ANIICA and, for this reason, is of great
importance to me, to you, to the people of Alaska, and to all t
citizens of the United States. Please advise me as to your
thoughts on anything I might do to further this acquisition.

With best regards,

Sincerely,

Cecil D. Andrus

P.S. Rest assured, the owner has access rights and an airfield.
If they sell to a developer, it will be one with the resources
to obtain water and other necessities.

cc: U.S. Senator Lisa Murkowski
    U.S. Representative Don Young
    Governor Frank Murkowski

FAX:202-224-2354
Original mailed

# Letter #4: Cecil D. Andrus to Senator Ted Stevens, 3/30/2006

CECIL D. ANDRUS

March 30, 2006

Senator Ted Stevens
United States Senate
522 Hart Building
Washington, D.C. 20510-0201

Dear Senator:

Thank you and your staff for the prompt response to my inquiry about the Orange Hill property inside the Wrangell-St. Elias National Park. I recognize that an easement for this acquisition of private property inside the Park is out of the question in the current environment in Washington. I wouldn't even ask you to take that action. I would respectfully request, however, that you keep the heat on the National Park Service to do what they agreed to do years ago, and that was to complete the appraisal of the property and thus to acquire it as was set forth in the ANILCA EIS Record of Decision, which said "to acquire all claims." This acquisition could come from current ISPS funding.

The reason for our concern at this point in time is that, after 25 years of coordinate and substantial investment by Mr. McGregor and his associates to convey this property to the National Park Service, they have become frustrated by the lack of action and have hired a professional marketing group to solicit potential purchasers for the development of his mineralized property.

Pursuant to your request, Senator, I will talk to my friends at The Nature Conservancy and in other organizations to see whether we can create any interest in trying to pick up this property and to protect it until the NPS acts.

Thanks again for your prompt attention to this matter.

With best regards,

Sincerely,

Cecil D. Andrus

# Appendix A: An Alaskan Hall of Heroes

## A Partial List of Those Who Helped

"Success has a thousand fathers. Failure is a bastard."
---former Interior Secretary Cecil D. Andrus

Any attempt at compiling this kind of list is fraught with the risk that some deserving and worthy folks will be left off purely by accident. To those deserving and worthy folks I want to apologize. I accept sole responsibility for this list and the reader has my assurance that I consulted others. I also was fortunate that Chuck Clusen had a list that he and some others in the Alaska Coalition compiled for a tenth anniversary event held by the Coalition in Washington, D.C., in 1990.

As the 35th anniversary of President Carter signing the most sweeping conservation act in the nation's history approaches, I am struck by how many on this list have already departed for the Big National Park in the Sky, where one hopes they can hike the many trails they did not have time for on this side of the veil of tears.

President Carter is approaching 90 and Secretary Andrus turned 84 in August while still holding folks accountable. Senator Ted Stevens has passed on, as has Harry Crandell, Mo Udall, Scoop Jackson, Paul Tsongas, Jay Hammond, Bill Egan and numerous other players on the Alaska stage.

The "Big 3" of the Alaska Coalition—Chuck Clusen, Brock Evans and Doug Scott—are either in their 70s or rapidly approaching the Biblical three score and ten.

Many on the list will or would have declined the honor of being cited as a hero, content to have quietly, professionally and competently done their part. Success was reward enough with no need of recognition. Still, perhaps for their children or grandchildren it will help validate for them that their forbears had a role in something so grand that it will be a gift and a legacy to many generations yet to come.

Truth be told, the people who belong on this list know who they are. No one needs to call their name for they know at an earlier time in their life they did answer a very special call.

Success in the cause of the Alaska lands legislation really did have a thousand fathers and mothers. I sincerely wish I could name all.

Some may also want to know what criteria I employed in deciding who went on the list. It was really rather basic: at the end of the day when all was said and done, did they act responsibly and constructively?

Thus, in my book Senator Stevens belongs on the list; Senator Gravel does not.


The Coach and the Quarterback:

President Jimmy Carter

Cecil D. Andrus, Secretary of the Interior


The White House team:

    Stuart Eizenstat, director of domestic policy

    Kathy Fletcher, assistant to Eizenstat and lead Interior liaison

    Frank Moore, director of congressional relations

        Jim Free, assistant for congressional relations

            Patricia Carroll, staff assistant

        Dan Tate, assistant for congressional relations

        Gary Fontana, assistant for congressional relations

    Hamilton Jordan, chief of staff

    Jody Powell, press secretary

    Jack Watson, director of communications

    Charles Kirbo, counselor to the President

    Anne Wexlar, director of community outreach

Bob Bergland, Secretary of the Dept. of Agriculture
Former Interior Secretary Rogers C.B. Morton
Former Interior Secretary Fred Seaton

The Interior Department team:
Jim Joseph, Undersecretary
Guy Martin, A/S for Land and Water
Dan Beard, Dpty A/S for Land and Water
Bob Herbst, A/S for Fish, Wildlife and Parks
David Hales, Dpty A/S for Fish, Wildlife and Parks
Joan Davenport, Asst. Secretary for Energy & Minerals
R.J. Bruning, Special Asst to the A/S
Steve Quarles
Jim Webb
Diane Josephy
Juanita Alvarez
Nat Reed, Former Asst. Secretary for Fish, Wildlife & Parks

Office of the Secretary Alaska Task Force:
Cynthia Wilson, Director
Sue Kemnitzer
Jim Pepper
Marilou Reilly
Jerry Gilliland, Director of Secretary's Alaskan Office
John D. Hough, Western Field, Office of the Secretary
Chris Carlson, assistant to secretary, director office of public affairs
Harmon Kallman, deputy director, Office of Public Affairs
Mark Panitch, Special assistant for Alaska affairs
Joe Nagel, assistant to the Secretary for state relations
Gary Catron, assistant to secretary, director of office of legislative and congressional affairs

John Powell
Chip Markell
John Gingles
Sarge Carleton
Tom Reed
Bill Aycock
Jane Lyder
Chuck Parrish, chief of staff
Jay Wade, executive secretary
Gordon Law
Jay Hakes

Solicitor's Office:
Leo Krulitz, solicitor
Clyde Martz
Fred Ferguson
Molly Ross
Tom Lundquist
Chuck Kaiser
Alice Herter
Paul Kirton
Dave Grayson
Dave Watts
Gary Widman
Don Barry
John Leshy, assistant solicitor

National Park Service:
Bill Whalen, former director
Russ Dickenson, director
George Hartzog, former director

Roger Contor, northwest regional director

| | |
|---|---|
| Mike Lambe | Ray Bane |
| Randy Jones | George Collins |

| | |
|---|---|
| John Cook | Mike Finley |
| Bob Belous | Paul Fritz |
| Chuck Gilbert | William Everhat |
| Ted Swam | Dick Stenmark |
| Bailey Breedlove | Carol Breedlove |
| Ira Hutchison | Harry Thomas, Jr. |
| John Kauffman | John Reynolds |

U.S. Fish & Wildlife Service:
Lynn Greenwalt, director
Bill Reffalt
Christine Enright

| | |
|---|---|
| Burke Neely | Dave Spencer |
| Jay Walker | David Cline |
| Dick Nadeau | Larry Means |
| Sandra Redeagle | John Gottschalk |
| Will Troyer | Fran Mauer |

BLM
Frank Gregg, director
Jim Scott
Wayne Boden
Julie Tilosten

Other Interior Notables:
Bill Menard
Chris Delaport
John Haubert

Curtis (Buff) Bohlen
Douglas Wheeler
Peter Tonnessen
John Farrell
Don Mitchell
Stan Sloss
Deborah Van Hoffman
Dave McCraney
Michael Hood
Peg Rosenberry
Marge Kimura
Barbara Mack-Heller

Environmental Protection Agency:
George Alderson
Bill Reilly

Department of Justice:
  Sandy Sagalkin
  Steve Herman
  Jim Brokshire
Lois Schiffer
Kay Oberly

State of Alaska
  Governor Jay Hammond
  Governor Bill Egan
  AG Av Gross
  AG John Havelock
  John Katz
  Stan Senner

Bill Horn
Tom Meachem
Dick Alman
Walt Parker
Patrick Dobby
Pat Pourchot

Members and Staff of the U.S. House:

Representative Morris Udall of Arizona
    Charles Conklin, Interior committee staff director
    Stanley Scoville, House Interior committee staff
    Mark Trautwein, committee staff
    Melanie Beller
    Lee McElvain
    Roy Jones
    Fran Sheahan
Representative John Seiberling of Ohio
    Loretta Neumann, committee staff
    Harry Crandell, committee staff
    Andy Wiessner, committee staff
    Stan Sloss
    Dennis Morfield
    Betsy Cuthbertson
    Kay Castevens
    Wilda Chisholm
Representative Syd Yates of Illinois
Mary Bain, Representative Yates' chief of staff
Representative John Anderson of Illinois
Representative Lloyd Meeds of Washington
Representative Norm Dicks of Washington
Representative Al Swift of Washington

Representative Don Clausen of California
Representative Phil Burton
    Jan Mooday
Representative Joe Fisher of Virginia
Representative Nick Begich of Alaska
Representative John Saylor of Pennsylvania
Representative Tom Foley of Washington
Representative Jim Weaver of Oregon
Representative Goodloe Byron of Maryland
Representative Allen Steelman of Texas
Representative Pete McCloskey of California
Representative Teno Roncalio of Wyoming
Representative Tom Evans of Virginia
Representative Bruce Vento of Minnesota
    Rick Healy
    Larry Romans

Members and staff of the U.S. Senate:

Senator Ted Stevens of Alaska
    Celia Niemi, executive assistant
Senator Henry Jackson of Washington
    Denny Miller, chief of staff
Dan Dreyfus, staff director, Senate Energy committee
Bill van Ness, chief counsel to Senate Interior Committee
Mike Harvey, staff counsel
Senator Paul Tsongas of Massachusetts
    Richard Arenberg, staff aide
Senator Dale Bumpers of Arkansas
Senator J. Bennett Johnston of Louisiana
Senator Dennis DeConcini of Arizona

Senator Alan Bible of Nevada
Senator George McGovern of South Dakota
Senator Lee Metcalf of Montana
    Ted Roe
Senator Gary Hart of Colorado
Senator John Durkin of New Hampshire
Senator Gaylord Nelson of Wisconsin
Senator Alan Cranston of California
    Kathy Lacey
    Roy Greenaway

Native American leaders and consultants:
John Borbridge, Tlingit-Haida Nation leader, AFN director
Byron Mallott, AFN director
Emil Notti, AFN director
Charley Edwardsen

| | |
|---|---|
| Willie Hensley | Matthew Fred |
| Bill Paul | Sarah James |
| Fred Paul | Willie Kasayulie |
| Eben Hopson | John Shively |
| Dave Friday | Jonathan Soloman |
| Willie Goodwin, Jr. | Robert Utley |

Media and writers:
John McPhee, author of *Coming Into the Country*
Mary Clay Berry, D.C. correspondent for the *Anchorage Times*
A. Robert Smith, D.C. correspondent for the *Anchorage Daily News*
Kay Fanning, publisher of the *Anchorage Daily News*
Lew Williams, publisher of the *Ketchikan Daily News* and the *Sitka Sentinel*
Joel Connelly, columnist for the *Seattle Post-Intelligencer*

Tim Egan, reporter and columnist for the *New York Times*
Phil Shabecoff, *New York Times*
Craig Medred, reporter for the *Juneau Southeast Alaska Empire*
Howard Rock, *Tundra Times*
Thomas Snapp, *Tundra Times*
Tom Brown, Editor, *Anchorage Daily News*
George Wills, columnist and author

| | |
|---|---|
| Margaret Murie | Richard Olson |
| Richard Conley | Richard Nelson |
| James Deane | Boyd Norton |
| Michael Frome | C. Don Mitchell |

The Alaska Coalition and Americans for Alaska
People:

| | |
|---|---|
| Chuck Clusen | Frances Beinecke |
| Doug Scott | Peter Berle |
| Brock Evans | Rex Blazer |
| Laurence Rockefeller, Jr. | Jim Blomquist |
| Mike McCloskey | Steve Hinniker |
| Joe Fontaine | Barbara Blum |
| Ed Wayburn | Stanley Boline |
| Russell Peterson | Mary Ellen Cuthbertson |
| Elvis Stahr | Ernie Day |
| Jack Hession | Ed Dayton |
| Dee Frankfourth | Peter Scholes |
| Alison Horton | Cecil Dickinson |
| Paul Peyron | Pat Robles |
| Bob Childers | Rich Gordon |
| Wendell Mohling | Alison Horton |
| Mrs. David "Mark" Hickock | Destry Jarvis |
| Carol Mohling | Chuck Johnstone |
| Steve Young | Dale Jones |

Winky Miller
Cathy Smith
David Klein
George Collins
Lowell Sumner
Olaus Murie
Robert Weeden
Rich Gordon
Joseph FitzGerald
Celia Hunter
David Hickok
George Marshall
Stewart Brandborg
Lloyd Tuppling
Richard Cooley
Pam Rich
Jim Kowalsky
Tim Stonorov
Eugene Knoder
Destry Jarvis
Brec Cooke
Barbara Blake
Story Clark
Carolyn Carr
Anna Grabowski
Dan Evans
Cathleen Douglas-Stone
James Buckley
Theodore Roosevelt IV
John Sherman Cooper
Henry Cabot Lodge
Tom Bradley

Sally Kabish
Sue Kemnitzer
Eugene Knodor
Bert Kochler
Tom Kouclaki
John Kintille
David Lavine
Bill Liensch
Jack Lorenz
Dan Lufkin
Tom McLeney
Bill Marks
Pat Noonan
John Adams
Robert Allan
Ben Childers
Lon Clapper
Gene Coon
Polly Dyer
Jonathan Ela
David Finkelstein
Barry Flam
Dee Frankforth
Vicki Frankforth
Greashoyh
Barbara Haas
Tony Heinult
Jay Hair
Bruce Hamilton
Mary Hanley
Linda Haverfield
Ron Hawk

| | |
|---|---|
| Douglass Fraser | Hans Neuhaser |
| Marshall Field | Sharon Neorand |
| Leonard Firestone | Dave Ortman |
| Louis Lundborg | Willa Parker |
| Roy Larsen | Mrs. Marlon Perkins |
| Terry Sanford | Max Peterson |
| George Romney | Paul Payton |
| General Mathew Ridgeway | Cleve Pinnix |
| Admiral Elmo Zumwalt | Paul Pritchard |
| Vernon Jordan | Sally Raney |
| Orville Freeman | E.G. Beckley |
| Eliot Porter | Don Redford |
| Hans Bethe | Ann Roosevelt |
| Paul Nitze | James Rush |
| George Schlesren | Denise Schlesren |
| Charles Mitchell | Lisa Schmidt |
| Matthew Scott | Ben Shiver |
| Bill Mankin | George Shelben |
| Miriam Steel | Metherd Sharpe |
| Al Stanley | John Sheahan |
| Ken McClaugherry | Dean Shirer |
| Randy Snodgrass | Ted Stanley |
| Karen Tilberg | Russel Train |
| Dora Youel | Will Troyer |
| Sandy Turner | Larry Williams |
| Reuben Wodder | Ginny Wood |
| Esther Wunniki | Jane Yern |
| Brooks Yeager | Ellie Bolton Kelly |
| David Borden | Chip Bevins |
| David Brower | William Brown |
| Pam Bryson | John Bryant |

Brent Calkins

Charles Callison

Carolyn Carr

Mike Metz

John McComb

Ran McCullough

Mike McIntosh

Rita Molyneaux

James Moorman

Anne Morton

Organizations:

Alaska Center for the Environment

Alaska Conservation Society

American Institute of Architects

American League of Anglers

American Littoral Society

American Rivers Conservation Council

Americans for Democratic Action

Appalachian Mountains Club

Arctic International Wildlife Range Society

Brooks Range Trust

Center for Action on Endangered Specie

The Cousteau Society

Defenders of Wildlife

Denali Citizens Council

Environmental Action

Environmental Defense Fund

Environmental Policy Center

Fairbanks Environmental Center

Federation of Fly Fisherman

Federation of Western Outdoors Clubs

Friends of the Earth

The Garden Clubs of America

International Backpackers Association

International Ecology Society

International Association of Machinists and Aerospace Workers
National Audubon Society
National International Recreational Sports Association
National Land for People
National Parks and Conservation Association
National Recreation and Park Association
National Speleological Society
National Wildlife Refuge Association
Natural Resources Defense Council
North American Wildlife Park Foundation
Oil, Chemical and Atomic Workers International
The Ozark Society
Public Lands Institute
Rivers Unlimited
Sierra Club
Southeast Alaska Conservation Council
Trout Unlimited
Trumpeter Swan Society
Trustees for Alaska
United Automobile Workers of America
United Electrical, Radio and Machine Workers
United Mine Workers of America
United Steelworkers of America
The Wilderness Society
Wilderness Watch
Wolf Sanctuary
World Wildlife Fund
And other supporting organizations included:
Americans for Alaska
Izaak Walton League of America
National Wildlife Federation

# Bibliography

Andrus, Cecil D. (with Joel Connelly), *Politics: Western Style*, Sasquatch Books, Seattle, 1995.

Berry, Mary Clay, *The Alaska Pipeline*, Indiana University Press, Bloomington, 1975.

Bovard, James, *Lost Rights: The Destruction of American Liberty*, St. Martin's Griffin, New York, 1994.

Brinkley, Douglas, *The Quiet World*, Harper, New York, 2011.

Gardey, Jon, *Alaska: The Sophisticated Wilderness*, Stein & Day, New York, 1976.

Greiner, James. *Wager With the Wind*, Rand McNally & Co., Chicago, 1974.

Gruening, Ernest, *Many Battles*, Liveright, New York, 1973.

Hanrahan, John, *Lost Frontier*, W.W. Norton, New York, 1977.

Hunt, William R., *Alaska: A Bicentennial History*, W.W. Norton, New York, 1976.

Lopez, Barry, *Arctic Dreams*, Charles Scribner's Sons, New York, 1986.

McGinniss, Joe, *Going to Extremes*, Alfred A. Knopf, New York, 1980.

McPhee, John, *Coming Into the Country*, Farrar, Straus and Giroux, New York, 1976.

Norton, Boyd, *Alaska: Wilderness Frontier*, Readers' Digest Press, New York, 1977.

Stahr, Walter, *Seward: Lincoln's Indispensable Man*, Simon & Schuster, New York, 2012.

Turner, James Morton, *The Promise of Wilderness*, University of Washington Press, Seattle, 2012.

**Articles and Periodicals**
*Anchorage Daily News*
*Anchorage Times*
*Ketchikan Daily News*
*Spokesman-Review*
*Southeast Alaska Empire*
*Los Angeles Times*
*Newsweek*
*St. Louis Post-Dispatch*
*New York Times*
*The Idaho Statesman*
*The Lewiston Tribune*
*Seattle Post-Intelligencer*
*Seattle Times*
*Wall Street Journal*
*Washington Post*

Cahn, Bob, *The Fight to Save Wild Alaska*, Audubon Magazine, 1981.

Andrus, Cecil, *President Carter's Coup* (Chapter 6), The Antiquities Act (edited by David Harmon), University of Arizona Press, Tucson, 2006.

*Almanac of American Politics 2008* (edited by Michael Barone), Alaska, National Journal, Washington, D.C., 2008

Haycox, Stephen W., *The Politics of Environment: Cecil Andrus and the Alaska Lands*, Idaho Yesterdays, Fall, 1992 issue (Judith Austin, editor), Boise, 1992.

Johnson, Marc, Four Taped Interviews with Cecil Andrus on Alaska, transcripts (unpublished), February/March, 1993, Boise.

Whitney, David, Ted Stevens: Big Voice for Alaska, 7-part series, *Anchorage Daily News*, August 7-10, 1994, Anchorage.

Burnett, Robert M. (editor), *Alaska Blue Book 1977*, Alaska Dept. of Education, Juneau, 1977.

**About the author**

Chris Carlson has a "checkered past." Born in Kellogg on December 22, 1946, the eldest son of two school teachers, the family moved to the Spokane Valley when he was ten. During teenage summers he held a variety of jobs, from being the town dry cleaner in Salmon to opening old collapsed mine tunnels near Idaho's Big Horn Crags to working in the woods of north Idaho as a choke-setter and tree-faller.

He graduated from Central Valley High School in 1965 and attended Columbia on a scholarship where he received his B.A. in three years by taking the maximum course loads allowed and attending summer school. He majored in English Literature and minored in Comparative Religions. Upon graduation in May of 1968 and facing the prospect of the draft, he took ten education credits at Gonzaga which qualified him for an Idaho provisional teaching certificate. He secured a position teaching 8th and 9th grade classes at Kootenai Junior-Senior High School and also coached the junior varsity basketball team.

In the fall of 1969 he began work on his M. A. in English Literature at Idaho State University where he also taught two sections of Freshman Composition each semester. Planning to marry in June of 1970 and needing more money he secured an additional full-time job as the political and education reporter for Pocatello's daily newspaper, the *Idaho State Journal*. Completing his M.A. in just one academic year, he decided to pursue a journalism career and worked for six short months for the *Spokane Daily Chronicle*.

In January of 1970 he became the chief correspondent in Washington, D.C., for the *Anchorage Daily News*. While there he also began writing a weekly political column carried by five newspapers in his native Idaho. After two years, he began a thus far life-long association with Idaho Governor Cecil D. Andrus, and returned to Idaho to become the governor's press secretary. Five years later he returned to Washington, D.C., as the Assistant Secretary of the Interior for Public Affairs when Andrus became Interior Secretary during the presidency of Jimmy Carter.

In January of 1981 Governor John Evans named him to the newly created Northwest Power Planning Council. In November, he resigned to begin his private sector career, first as vice president of The Rockey Company, a Seattle-based public relations firm, where he set up the firm's public affairs division. In November of 1984 he was lured back to Spokane by the then area's largest private employer, Kaiser Aluminum, which made him the vice president for northwest public affairs. In January of 1989 he left to be the founding partner and open the Spokane office of what would become the region's largest independent public affairs firm, The Gallatin Group, with offices in Boise, Seattle, Portland and Helena as well as Spokane.

Upon leaving the governorship in January of 1995, Cecil Andrus, with whom he remained associated, accepted his offer to join The Gallatin Group as a Senior of Counsel and operate from the firm's Boise office.

In 1999, Chris was diagnosed with Parkinson's disease which mercifully has moved very slowly and is still confined to his left side. He continued to run the Spokane office and serve on Gallatin's board. In November of 2005, however, he was diagnosed with late Stage IV carcinoid neuroendocrine cancer and given six months to live. The world's premier hospital for this form of cancer, Houston's M.D. Anderson, after looking at his CAT scans and MRI's, refused to see him to give a second opinion. He then turned to the Huntsman Cancer Institute at the

University of Utah in Salt Lake City where he underwent a series of chemoembolization procedures including an experimental last one in which radioactive pellets were placed on the remnants of shattered tumors on his liver. He also receives a monthly sandostatin shot. For whatever reason his cancer stabilized and he is still here defying the odds.

He took a medical disability retirement from his firm but has remained active in the public arena. He chaired the 2008 campaign in Washington state against Initiative 1000, the doctor assisted suicide measure.

He writes a weekly political column carried by three papers and two blog sites in Idaho. He is the author of *Cecil Andrus: Idaho's Greatest Governor* and *Medimont Reflections*, a book of essays on other notable Idahoans and issues he has dealt with over a 40 year career.

He and his wife, Marcia, were married on June 12, 1970, and now reside at Medimont on Cave Lake in southern Kootenai county. They have four adult children and two grandchildren and attend St. Augustine's Catholic Church in Spokane.

CPSIA information can be obtained at www.ICGtesting.com
Printed in the USA
LVOW07s0456140116

469957LV00005B/9/P